Odets
the Playwright

The front cover photo of Clifford Odets
is by Alfredo Valente and is reproduced
by courtesy of the Odets Estate and
the Robert A. Freedman Dramatic Agency, Inc.

Other Modern Theatre Profiles

Odets
the Playwright

GERALD WEALES

METHUEN · LONDON AND NEW YORK

A Methuen Paperback

First published in 1985 as a Methuen Paperback original
by Methuen London Ltd, 11 New Fetter Lane, London EC4P 4EE
and Methuen Inc, 733 Third Avenue, New York, NY 10017.

An earlier version of this book, under the title
Clifford Odets – Playwright, was published in 1971
in the United States of America only by Bobbs-Merrill.
Copyright © 1971, 1985 by Gerald Weales
Printed in Great Britain
by Richard Clay (The Chaucer Press) Ltd,
Bungay, Suffolk

Weales, Gerald
    Odets the playwright.—(Methuen modern theatre
    profile series)
    1. Odets, Clifford—Criticism and interpretation
    I. Title
    812´.54   PS3529.D46Z/

ISBN 0-413-58020-2

Contents

Acknowledgments

I want to thank the New York Public Library, particularly the staff of the Theatre Collection at Lincoln Center where I set up housekeeping for so many days; the Library of Congress where I read most of the unpublished plays of Odets and saw a number of the movies he wrote or directed; those members of the University of Pennsylvania Library staff who helped me track down arcane facts and obscure books; the Philadelphia *Bulletin*, which let me use its clip files; Mark Goodson of Goodson-Todman Productions, who arranged for me to see the typescripts of the Odets television plays; Nora Magid and Hope Davis, who read my first draft and made practical suggestions; and, most of all, Yaddo where the book was written.

G.W.

Clifford Odets – Chronology

1906 Born 18 July. Philadelphia.

1923 Drops out of high school.

1924–28 Theatrical odd-jobbery: acts in small companies in New York and Philadelphia, works in radio.

1929–30 Understudies Spencer Tracy in *Conflict*. Bit parts in Theatre Guild road companies. Featured in Claire and Paul Sifton's *Midnight*.

1931 Joins newly formed Group Theatre. Plays minor roles in Group productions through 1934.

1933 Last non-Group role (a lead finally) in *They All Came to Moscow*.

1934 Joins Communist Party. Unjoins after a few months but remains sympathetic.

1935 *Waiting for Lefty* introduces Odets as playwright. *Awake and Sing!* opens. *Lefty* moves to Broadway on double bill with *Till the Day I Die*. Writes "I Can't Sleep" for Morris Carnovsky. *Paradise Lost* opens.

1936 Goes to Hollywood. Writes *The General Died at Dawn*.

1937 Marries Luise Rainer. *Golden Boy* opens.

1938 *Rocket to the Moon* opens.

1940 *Night Music* opens.

1941 *Clash by Night* opens.

1942 *The Russian People* opens.

1943 Marries Bette Grayson.

1944 Writes and directs *None But the Lonely Heart*.

1946 *Deadline at Dawn* released.

1947 *Humoresque* released. Show of watercolours in New York.

1949 *The Big Knife* opens.

1950 *The Country Girl* opens.

1951 Divorce from Bette Grayson.

1952 Testifies before House Un-American Activities Committee.

1954 *The Flowering Peach* opens.

1957 *Sweet Smell of Success* released.

1960 *The Story on Page One* released.

1961 *Wild in the Country* released.

1962–63 Works on musical version of *Golden Boy* (re-written by William Gibson, produced 1964). Writes scripts and acts as story editor for NBC-TV dramatic series "The Richard Boone Show" (two of his scripts broadcast after his death, 1963–1964).

1963 Dies 14 August. Los Angeles.

Green in nature is one thing, green
in literature another —

Virginia Woolf, *Orlando*

I. *"Somebody to Be Reckoned With"*

> A new Odets has come to town. I see him as a suit of my
> clothes with some utter stranger inside them, who is known
> as 'Odets, the successful playwright,' and who receives fan-
> tastic offers from Hollywood, invitations to address ladies'
> clubs, one hundred and fifty telephone calls a day and a lot
> of solemn consideration from guys who write pieces for the
> dramatic page.

So Clifford Odets told A. J. Liebling in an interview which
at once diagnosed and fed the sudden attack of notoriety which
had struck the young playwright. The suit, according to Liebling, was a thirty-five-dollar gray number which Odets wore
with "a blue broadcloth shirt, slightly frayed at the collar"; the
photograph accompanying the story was a standard publicity
shot of a far too pretty Odets, his wild hair carefully tamed and
his collar looking not at all frayed. The illustration—like the
interview, like the pseudo-biography that Odets trotted out at
the drop of a question—somewhat muddies the classic picture
of Odets as the young talent raped by success; he was willing,
even eager.

Although that willingness gives a certain ambiguity to his later plays about the pitfalls of success (*Golden Boy*, *The Big
Knife*), it does not materially affect the Broadway ritual he was
beginning to act out in 1935. Season after season, surprised to
find talent in the American theater, the reviewers, the columnists, the editors (and now the media culture specialists) discover
new playwrights and new performers to tout—headache reme-
dies sold as cancer cures—and the celebrity users descend on
the newcomers and beat them to death with invitations. At
least, most of them die off quickly. Although it would be
difficult to find a young talent that did not go skipping to that

11

sacrifice, the hardier ones—Tennessee Williams, say, or Edward Albee—refuse simply to succumb to the offered material and social rewards; they take the applause, guy the givers and go on trying to create themselves as artists, to make careers solid enough to detach the labels pasted on them with their first success. Clifford Odets belongs with the hardy ones.

At the time of the Liebling interview, Odets had three plays running on Broadway—*Awake and Sing!* and the double bill, *Waiting for Lefty* and *Till the Day I Die*—and another promised for the fall. Although none of them were commercial successes, they created the "new Odets" of the Liebling story. "For me, strangely enough, the success and fame was a source of acute discomfort," Odets told an interviewer in 1961, ". . . you don't want to change, you want to hold on . . . but you're just kind of swept off your feet, with wire services and interviews and people telephoning you; the parties you're invited to, the people who just take you up." In *The Fervent Years,* Harold Clurman recalls those days, when the phone in the apartment he shared with Odets never stopped ringing: "Odets was in a whirl, pleasant at first no doubt, a little terrifying later." After all, one is not simply toasted on the celebrity circuit; one is eaten, too. In his "So This is Broadway" column, George Ross gave a hint of the pleasure and the terror:

> They spoke last year [he means *last season*] of the emergence of a flaming playwright, of the Theater's White Hope, of the new O'Neill, and they were speaking this year, in the same circles and in whispers and in less reverent tones, of Clifford Odets. . . . had been seen with Tallulah Bankhead, had been noticed talking to Beatrice Lillie, who is a Lady, at somebody's midnight social, had been observed at Fire Island week-ending with Fannie Brice, the Gershwins, Gene Fowlers and the like. . . . "Will Odets," it often was asked at numerous soirees, "keep his head after all that acclaim or will he go in for social climbing, Hollywood and cocktails at five?"

Ross's column was a defense of Odets against those whispers, an insistence that he was still unspoiled, busily working on his plays. But in a gossip column there is no security in a defense:

"Nor is he contaminated by the lucre and lustre every time he enters Tony's or Twenty-One. Which he does."

For a secular society, the United States is remarkably preoccupied with the Fall. Implicit in the celebration of any writer (of any man) is the assumption that the celebration itself corrupts and that the wages of sin will be immediately apparent—in the next book, the next play. For that reason, Odets, as celebrity, cannot be separated from Odets, the playwright. The latter made the former and, so the cliché goes, the former wrecked the latter. All the talk about where Odets was seen with whom was no more than a distorted reflection of the enthusiasm with which the young playwright's work was received. Not that his critical reception was ever unmixed. Still, the prevailing attitude assumed that he was, in the words and capitals of *Town and Country*, "Somebody to Be Reckoned With." At a less gushy level, Archibald MacLeish wrote, "Now the point I am trying to make is not that Clifford Odets is a good playwright nor that his work is better than anything else in New York. The first fact is pretty widely known and the second is obvious."

What happens to the young playwright when the serious and the trivial join forces to declare his preeminence? Even if he were no more vain than the rest of the breed, a certain self-assurance might well surface. "I am the most talented young playwright in the business," he told a New York *Times* interviewer, only slightly qualifying the remark with "because play writing has reached a sad state and there are no talented writers today." "I am your playwriting son!" he is supposed to have written, demanding that George Bernard Shaw pay attention to him, but the authority here is George Jean Nathan, and Nathan made a practice of trying to cut Odets down to size. When the Leftist playwright in the Edna Ferber-George S. Kaufman *Stage Door* (1936) meets the heroine in Act I, he says that his "was the best goddam play that was ever produced in New York! And the one I'm writing now is even better." Little wonder that that brash young man, who talked a good proletarian line until success forced him into a dinner jacket and finally sent him to Hollywood, was said to be based on Odets.

Cheeky quotations (or mis-quotations) are one thing, but it was Broadway hubris that forced Odets to attempt to educate

13

the reviewers by sending around an explanation of his *Paradise Lost* just before the play opened in December 1935. The scene was set for a deflation. *Paradise Lost* was roasted. Odets ran—to Hollywood. For the next twenty-eight years, he was going to be nagged by 1935. He became the revolutionary playwright who quit making revolutions, the promising playwright who never kept his promises. Not that the celebrity ended. As late as the 1940s, Cole Porter used him in two of his name-dropping songs—"I'm Throwing a Ball Tonight" (*Panama Hattie*, 1940) and "Farming" (*Let's Face It*, 1941)—although in the first instance the choice may have been dictated by the need for a rhyme for *regrets*. Not that the publicity stopped. After the success of *Golden Boy*, Odets was the subject of a *New Yorker* profile and a *Time* cover story.

But the reaction had already set in. The more venomous critics, of whom Grenville Vernon is a good if unimportant example, tried to exorcise Odets by dismissing his work and denying the force of 1935. In a very petulant appraisal of the Odets plays through *Golden Boy*, Vernon went so far as to accuse Odets of dishonesty in trying to pass himself off as an important American playwright:

> In the drama the shrillest horn-blower of them all is Clifford Odets. Mr. Odets is certainly determined not to let die the legend that he is the White Hope of the American theatre. Not even living in Hollywood and receiving the shekels of the mammon of the movies, has daunted his faith in himself. And by blowing his horn hard enough he has convinced a few otherwise sensible critics that the Hope has become a Reality.

More significant is the tone of voice among the sensible critics. Reviewers, even when they praised a play, could scarcely keep from treating Odets as an historical character who, way back in 1935, reflected so accurately the intellectual tone of the time (a moment when art and politics shared the stage) and who seemed about to blossom into that great American playwright who is presumably always in the wings. "It is not fair to make esteem for the work of a writer's ardent youth a lien on his entire life," John Gassner wrote, but the line appears in a review of *The*

14

Country Girl, in which Gassner keeps harping back to the earlier Odets. "In this country, a playwright is a genius in May and an idiot in December," Odets once told an interviewer from the Baltimore *Sun,* "—the white hope of the drama at the age of 26 and a bum when he is 35."

One of the problems in writing about Odets, then, is to keep him from dwindling into that familiar American stereotype, the flash-in-the-pan, the early success who goes sour. He was, after all, a man who spent thirty years writing plays, movies and, finally, television scripts; although his work is uneven and none of it is unflawed, he turned out a body of plays that can stand with the best that the American stage has produced. My emphasis on the playwright's whole career and my refusal to stick to the sentimental scenario of artistic virtue seduced are not attempts to deny the importance of Odets's flamboyant debut as a dramatist. His initial success obviously colored both his own and critics' attitudes toward his later work.

Aside from what that success did to (or for) him, it marks a memorable point in the history of American drama and American literature in general. *Awake and Sing!,* following hard on the heels of *Waiting for Lefty,* heralded another of the new beginnings which the American theater constantly undergoes. Although Odets's politics, his milieu, even his language have precedents in American drama—particularly among earlier Group Theatre writers such as John Howard Lawson—he came as a happy surprise to audiences, made the familiar seem suddenly fresh. The result, of course, was the kind of excitement indicated by the quotations that open this chapter. Once the publicity froth had drained off, however, an image of the decade still remained. Odets is so identified with the 1930s that a mention of his name elicits stock responses, the recollection of a time when literature was a weapon and leftist optimism almost mandatory. The young Odets has the force of a representative man, a fact that can best be illustrated by seeing how he and his early plays have been used by other writers. Sometimes it is no more than a label, a shorthand identification of a character or situation, as in John O'Hara's *The Champagne Pool* and Norman Mailer's *The Naked and the Dead.* In the O'Hara play, Joe Rasmussen, the Method-y director, says,

"When I was at Harvard I wrote a play that was such a steal from *Awake and Sing!* that I got embarrassed and called it a parody." In an anachronistic scene in the Mailer novel (right for the author's years at Harvard, wrong for the character's), a student with "a deep important voice" tries to convince the Dramatic Club that it should do Odets because "he's the only playwright in America who's doing anything serious, at least he has his feet in the frustrations and aspirations of the common people." Sometimes the Odets reference is more functional. In Irwin Shaw's "The Eighty-Yard Run," it is Darling's refusal to go to a performance of *Waiting for Lefty* that makes Louise recognize how far apart the two of them have grown. In James Baldwin's *Tell Me How Long the Train's Been Gone,* Leo Proudhammer and Barbara King choose to do for their audition "The Young Hack and His Girl" scene from *Lefty* and discover, as the obtuse director cannot, how relevant it is to their own racial-sexual situation. Even as far away as Belfast, Odets is a symbol of revolution: Gavin Burke, in Brian Moore's *The Emperor of Ice-Cream,* growing up and away from his family, joins the Grafton Players in their production of *Till the Day I Die,* less in quest of an ideal than in search of sin.

I know that there is something pretentious about the paragraph above, as though I were insisting on the catholicity of my reading, but it has its uses—for me, at least. I wanted to remind myself of the very real existence of Odets as idea before I moved on into the book in which, as I talk about his life and work, the mythic figure will necessarily give way to the man and the playwright.

II. *"Honestly, Clifford, unless you turn out to be a genius, no one will ever speak to you"*

HIS NAME WAS ODET, without the 's," Clifford Odets said of his father in an interview with Thomas Sugrue. "Someone spelled it wrong on a union card one day when he was looking for a job as a printer. To get it corrected he would have had to step out of line and lose his place. So he stayed in line and our name got an 's." It is an attractive story, straight out of the fact and folklore of American immigration, in which so many European names were accidentally altered by officials whose ears were attuned to nothing more exotic than English or Irish patronymics. It may even be true, but the Sugrue piece is scattered with the kind of misinformation ("Both my parents were born in Philadelphia") which suggests that either the subject or the interviewer was shaping the material for the occasion. It was, after all, written as a play: "Mr. Odets Regrets A Social Drama in One Act."

Certainly, the father's name was Louis Odets on the registration of Clifford's birth, on file with the Philadelphia Department of Records; not that the document is totally trustworthy since it spells the mother's maiden name (Geisinger) with two *s*'s. Clifford was born on July 18, 1906, the first child of a twenty-year-old Russian immigrant and his nineteen-year-old bride, Pearl, a native of Austria. He was born in a three-story red brick house, familiar Philadelphia row style, flush against the sidewalk with two steps in front, which was still standing at 207 George Street when I drove by to have a look at it in summer 1969. The street, only three blocks long, is in the Northern Liberties, a sizable area fronting on the Delaware River; it had a heavy German-Jewish population in the middle of the nineteenth century, but by the 1880s the sons of the earlier immigrants had moved out, leaving homes and synagogues to the new arrivals from Eastern Europe. By the 1930s, another urban shift had taken place. Upward mobility had carried the Jews of the Northern Liberties out to the Oak Lane section in Northern Philadelphia and it was there, at 1721 Sixty-Eighth Avenue, that Louis Odets settled in the late 1920s when he returned to Philadelphia, after having made his own upward move in the Bronx.

In his testimony before the House Un-American Activities Committee, in an attempt to explain that it was personal experience not ideology that governed his social responses, Odets said, "my mother worked in a stocking factory in Philadelphia at the age of 11 and died a broken woman and an old woman at the age of 48." Much earlier, he had said, "I was a worker's son until the age of 12."

After 1935, when Odets became good copy, he told his story so often, to so many interviewers, altering facts to fit the occasion, that it is a little difficult to trace the steps in Louis Odets's career. He worked in print shops in Philadelphia and in the Bronx, where the family moved when Odets was two, and came to own his own shop there. From that, he apparently moved into direct mail advertising and, by the time he returned to Philadelphia, was a fairly prosperous businessman, holding an executive position in a Philadelphia firm. Odets told John McCarten that he lived near Beck and Longwood Avenues in the Bronx, "then a rather elegant section," in one of the three (four, according to Sugrue) elevator buildings that the Bronx could boast in those days. For all the working-class background that lay in the Odets family before Clifford's birth and in his childhood, there is obviously truth in his admission: "This boy was a very ordinary middle-class boy." This helps explain why, as a playwright, he was always most comfortable with middle-class characters.

Odets was not quite the "typical, typical, so typical" boy he called himself in *Current Biography,* at least so far as his school-ing was concerned. After having attended P.S. 52 in the Bronx, he entered Morris High School in September 1921. According to his record, which includes comments on initiative, habits and courtesy, he was, during his first term, a "helpful," "very" cour-teous boy with "good" habits. If the "uncertain recollection" of Arthur Klein can be trusted, Odets was much the same at the end of his sophomore year; Klein, who was Odets's prefect dur-ing his last full term at Morris, wrote me: "I think I remember a quiet, well-mannered, rather good-looking young man with dark, thick, wavy hair. I believe I recall his joy when he won either an oratorical contest or a declamation contest. Unfortunately, nothing else comes to mind." However quiet, however good his habits, Odets had had enough of formal education by the begin-ning of his junior year; he dropped out of school on November 13, 1923. "I thought high school was a waste of time," he told Sugrue, "though I liked biology and English, and I acted in all the plays and belonged to the literary club. I flunked all my mathematics." That's not quite the whole story. He flunked not only algebra, but Spanish and bookkeeping, and had to take drawing a second time. Whether he was an incipient poet breaking an establishment-imposed regime or simply a bored boy who could not face another year of classes, at the age of seventeen Odets stepped out into the big world.

It was not quite a giant step. Although Odets embarked on the traditional odd-jobbery years we have come to expect of the young writer or actor on his way up, he did not break with his family. Once they returned to Philadelphia, Odets moved back and forth between that city and New York, working now in one town, now in the other. His relations with his father were ap-parently a little stormy. At least, one of Odets's favorite stories is about the time his father, enraged that his son should want to be a poet rather than an advertising copywriter, smashed his typewriter. "Believe me, there were some very gloomy eve-nings," he was quoted in *Time,* which placed the event just after he left high school; when Sugrue told it, Odets was already act-ing in stock. Of course, the elder Odets replaced the typewriter —just as the father in *Humoresque,* past his initial fury, joined the mother in presenting the incipient prodigy with his first violin. Later, the Philadelphia *Record* quoted "proud Father Odets" as saying, "Clifford has talent enough for all."

Odets's mother was apparently a gentle woman; at least he took the trouble in later years to deny that *Awake and Sing!* was autobiographical, to differentiate between the tough Bessie and the historical Pearl. He told Seymour Peck, "My mother was a strange and nunlike woman who had to live with two brawling trigger-tempered men in the house—my father and myself." He also said that he burned all his pre-*Awake* writings ("This was the end of a whole period of my life"), a demonstrably false assertion since many of the early plays are extant. Aside from this suspect interview and his posthumous dedication of *Paradise Lost* ("For My Dead Mother") and *Six Plays* (1939) to her (the 1935 *Three Plays* was dedicated to both parents), there is little public evidence to indicate how close he may have been to her. In the Sugrue article, there is a strange statement about his mother's death which may be read as either a sign of the affection between them or as a kind of black comedy variation on the traditional Jewish mother (my son, the playwright). Mrs. Odets had died on May 8, 1935, at the height of her son's first success, and, so Odets presumably told Sugrue,

> it was really my success that brought her death. It excited her. It sent her off in ecstasies. Just before she died I showed her a picture of myself in a New York newspaper. She smiled and said, "It is good." That was the last thing she said to me.

Odets's two sisters—Genevieve (b. 1910) and Florence (b. 1917) —would still have been children when he left Morris High to make his way in the theater.

In 1938 the Odets home in Oak Lane was put up for a mortgage sale and drew no bidders. Some of the Philadelphia papers, trying to get a little human interest mileage out of a fairly commonplace event, made as much as they could of the successful playwright's allowing the old homestead to perish on the auction block. Since Odets had waived his share of his mother's estate ($3,031) two years earlier, it is likely that he could have come up with the mortgage money if anyone had wanted him to. His father and his sisters were the owners of the place on Sixty-Eighth Avenue and, since the girls were grown and the father lived at the Warwick Hotel, the sentimental attachment to Oak Lane was apparently minimal. Although big brother did not save the newspaper-invented day in 1938, he did look after his little sister in 1940. Florence, who had made her debut as an actress in a production of *Having Wonderful Time* at Brighton Beach in the year of the mortgage sale, had a bit part in her brother's *Night Music* and was one of the two assistant stage managers on the show. Hers was a brief theatrical career; as the elder Odets had said, Clifford was the one with talent in the family.

"Marx said it—abolish such families." This, from Jacob in *Awake and Sing!* Yet, whatever the theoretical shortcomings of the family, Odets's family portraits, from *Awake* to *The Flowering Peach* are marked by a querulous affection. From Ralph in *Awake* to Japheth in *Peach*, his young men try to escape their elders, knowing, as they struggle, that their trap is lined with love, however lethal. It is almost impossible to escape the biographical fallacy when talking about Odets's work; Harold Clurman in an obituary article on his friend, wrote, "The bulk of Odets's work was self-portrayal." If we can move backwards, from the plays to the man, it might be safe to assume that, particularly in the years before Odets found that artificial family, the Group Theatre, he kept returning to his own family for the affection and the impetus to escape that only a family can give. It is probably indicative of the detached attachment Odets had for his family that, in *The Fervent Years,* a book that is preoccupied with ways of belonging, there is only one specific reference to anyone in Odets's family; Clurman reports that Odets's father was upset when his son, made momentarily flush by an advance on a play, found himself an apartment adjoining a stable.

There was more than family to draw Odets back to Philadelphia. According to Richard Powell, Odets "used to come back to read his plays to friends and family and to argue over endless cups of coffee at a South Broad Street restaurant with his fellow radicals." When the Group brought *Awake and Sing!* and *Waiting for Lefty* to Philadelphia after the first New York run, there was a story in the Philadelphia *Record,* claiming that *Awake* had had its premiere in Philadelphia, that Odets had read it to a group of friends gathered in the home of Dr. M. V. Leof. Among the listeners were the Samuel Blitzsteins (he was father of composer Marc Blitzstein) and Mary and Joe Gerson, founders of the New Theatre, the home of radical drama in Philadelphia. Years later, Odets was to dedicate *The Big Knife* to Dr. Leof "in his seventy-eighth year, with love," and, I suspect, to put him in the play in the character of Dr. Frary. A more immediate and more ambiguous testimony to one of his Philadelphia friends can be found in the monologue, *I Can't Sleep* (1936); Odets calls his guilt-ridden speaker Sam Blitzstein. According to the *Record* story, some of that original gathering celebrated Odets's Philadelphia opening with a sentimental visit to that Broad Street restaurant "where 'Cliff', the reserved, almost taciturn young man with some decided views on the theater, used to meet with them to discuss art, the drama, music, politics and economics." Although there is a certain amount of fakery in the newspaper stories quoted above, the inevitable sentimentalization that accompanies memories of the local boy who made good, they do suggest that there was a community of sorts for Odets in Philadelphia, a circle of shared concerns, which was important to him during his formative years and to which he could return even after he had moved out into the wider circles of New York and Hollywood.

"I played in *What Price Glory?* with five stock companies and *An American Tragedy* with four stock companies." This hyperbolic statement (Odets to Sugrue) contains truth of a sort, even if one doubts that Odets played stock in "every city in the East." Once Odets let the doors of Morris High School close behind him, he did begin to try to make an actor of himself, working wherever he could find parts. He apparently began with the Drawing Room Players, an amateur group which performed one-act plays in the Heckscher Theatre, and later formed a group of his own, using Drawing-Room veterans. He acted with Harry Kemp's Poet's Theatre, which Kemp had started in 1925 after he had decided—along with Maxwell Bodenheim and some others—that Greenwich Village was too commercialized and had moved Bohemia east to Tompkins

Square. Kemp's theater, which performed in a chapel in St. Mark's-in-the-Bouwerie, failed, perhaps because the twenty-nine-cent admission charge did not bring in enough money to feed the herd of cows he kept to add atmosphere to some of his shows. If Odets had to risk being upstaged by a cow, he never mentioned it to interviewers. He did spend much of the time between 1925 and 1927 working in radio, a cowless medium. He was an announcer for a small station in the Bronx, and he once laid claim to having been the first disc jockey: "I used to play records all the time, and plug certain firms I made tie-ups with." He wrote two radio plays—*Dawn* and *At the Waterline* —the second of which was performed, with Odets in the lead, at radio stations in New York and Philadelphia. He billed himself as the Roving Reciter, offering Rudyard Kipling, Robert Service and other narrative poets. After he became well-known as a playwright, someone came across the actor's application he had once filed with NBC and passed it on to the New York *World-Telegram.* He claimed to be proficient in a wide variety of dialects—French, Jewish, Negro, Cockney, Irish, English, Russian, Chinese, and any regional American—but an unimpressed functionary at NBC noted, in a marginal entry, that he might be a possibility in French or Italian parts.

During the week of April 4, 1927, Clifford Odette turned up in two small roles in the production of *What Price Glory?* given by Mae Desmond and Her Players at the William Penn Theatre in Philadelphia. It was Louis Odet(s)'s name problem all over again and it was to stay with Odets until 1931. He was Odettes for Mae Desmond when he played Wild Tobe, the half-breed, in *Red Kisses* by Charles E. and H. Clay Blaney in January 1928. He was Odets for the rest of his stay with Mae Desmond and Her Players, but later in New York his name occasionally became Odetts, as in the Theatre Guild's *Roar China* and the first Group Theatre production, *The House of Connelly;* it was finally spelled correctly in the *Connelly* program for October 26, 1931, a month after the opening, and Clifford Odets, actor, was at last established, typographically at least.

There are precious few testimonials to Odets's acting and one of them—Mae Desmond's "I want you to know that I think you have talent"—is a little suspect. It comes to us third hand, from

John McCarten who apparently had it from Odets himself. Whether or not she actually paid him that compliment for his work in *What Price Glory?*, she obviously thought enough of him to have him in her company for the spring of 1928, although she wasted no major roles on him. Miss Desmond, an actress of some reputation before the first world war, settled in Philadelphia and with her husband (Frank Fielder) managed stock companies in that area from 1918 to 1931. The bills ran to melodrama, usually with a touch of the exotic and almost always with a choice part for Miss Desmond herself. During the first three months of 1928, besides his part in *Red Kisses*, Odets played two roles in Elinor Glyn's *Three Weeks*, Hendricks in John Willard's *The Cat and the Canary*, Tristan, the Captain of the Guard, in *The Hunchback of Notre Dame*, a lawyer in Bayard Veiller's *Within the Law*, Zoombie in *Kongo* by Chester Devonde and Kilbourne Gordon, two parts in *The Sins of the Rosary* and Judge John Billings in *Over the Hill to the Poorhouse*. Whether he had it or not, he could certainly have used the versatility he had tried to peddle to NBC; even later, in the first season of the Group, he had to play an elderly tenant farmer (one of Paul Green's "ancient ebony darkies") and a Mexican peasant, as well as a clutch of more conventional American characters.

Odets got a foothold on Broadway when he was signed to understudy Spencer Tracy, who played the lead in Warren F. Lawrence's *Conflict*. A drama about the marital problems of an aviator war hero, the play opened at the Fulton Theatre on March 6, 1929 and lasted for only thirty-seven performances, none of which Tracy missed. Even so, the production helped Odets's limping career. According to Burns Mantle, it was a member of the *Conflict* cast, Albert Van Dekker (he later dropped the *Van*), who introduced Odets to the Theatre Guild. He played one of the "Other Robots" in a road company production of *R.U.R.* that Rouben Mamoulian directed for the Guild in the fall of 1929. There is an anecdote in the McCarten profile on Odets about how the playwright rejected Mamoulian's suggestion that he do the screenplay for *Golden Boy* with these words: "You tell that - - that he is the only director I loathe and won't work with." This reaction presumably stemmed from the days of *R.U.R.* when Mamoulian supposedly vetoed a plan to give Odets a few lines with, "He is no good." The whole thing sounds a little like a standard come-uppance story and it came conveniently at the time when a number of columns carried conjectural items about whether or not Odets would adapt his successful play for the movies. Publicity ploy or true history, the story does have this basis in fact: Odets, who did not write the movie version of *Golden Boy*, had no lines in *R.U.R.* He was also an undifferentiated member of the crowd in *Marco Millions*, when that Guild show toured in January 1930. He stayed with the two shows when they came back to New York for brief runs in February *(R.U.R.)* and March *(Marco)*, and he turned up as one of the sailors on the H.M.S. *Europa* in *Roar China* in October of that year. Finally, on December 29, the young actor got to open his mouth when *Midnight*, a play by Claire and Paul Sifton, a melodrama with a social point, warning against too rigid adherence to the letter of the law, was produced at the Guild Theatre. Odets, who played the protagonist's son, was noticed by at least one reviewer; Percy Hammond called attention to him and Harriet MacGibbon "in minor roles completely understood and realized."

On September 28, 1931, the Group Theatre opened its initial production, Paul Green's *The House of Connelly*, in which all the minor Negro roles were filled by Group regulars. Odets, as Uncle Reuben, had to play a harmonica in one scene—or so he told Sugrue. Thus began, for Odets, a series of very tiny roles with the Group, too minor to attract the reviewers and finally very frustrating to his ambitions as an actor. He played several parts in the Siftons' *1931*—and Mateo in Maxwell Anderson's *Night Over Taos*. In the Group's second season, he understudied Luther Adler in the leading role of John Howard Lawson's *Success Story* and played a doorman in Dawn Powell's *Big Night*. When that play closed precipitately, ending the Group's season in January and threatening to end the Group itself, Odets went into his last non-Group production and his largest role in *They All Come to Moscow* by John Washburne and Ruth Kennell. One of a number of plays that set conventional genres against a Russian background, banking on a curiosity about all things Soviet *(Clear All Wires*, the 1932 farce by Sam and Bella Spewack is the successful example), *They All Come* was an unlikely triangle play in which Andrey, thinking that his Natalya is in love with an American engineer, is about to give her up when he discovers that, in fact, she loves him and all ends happily for the three friends. "Jack Davis serves modestly as the upright American engineer," wrote Burns Mantle, apparently without irony, and added, "Clifford Odets matches his nobility as the patriotic Russian husband." I am less certain about the innocence of Richard Lockridge's "Clifford Odets displayed great restraint," particularly when the line is placed alongside Arthur Pollock's judgment, "Clifford Odets is probably the best of the players, though he is practically inanimate." Describing his own acting to John McCarten five years later, Odets admitted, "I was too tense. . . . I couldn't relax." The New York *Times*'s L.N. dismissed the whole operation with "The Five-Year Plan and Love both took a nasty spill last evening," and the play folded after twenty performances.

When Sidney Kingsley's *Men in White*, the Group's first and biggest commercial success, opened on September 26, 1933, Odets was once again in a tiny role, playing Mr. Houghton, one of the hospital board that gives the idealistic doctor such a hard time. Years later, Leonard Lyons found Kingsley, Odets and Harold Clurman sitting around Sardi's reminiscing. Kingsley recalled an actor in *Men in White*, who kept adding a line ("Say, what are we, Boy Scouts?") to his part. "He kept putting it in, and I kept telling him that I was the playwright," Kingsley said. "Do you remember who did that?" Of course, Odets had to confess. "I remember. I did it." The anecdote appeared in the Lyons column for February 23, 1940, the day after *Night Music* opened, a convenient moment, in terms of publicity, for a recollection that Odets, the actor, was already an incipient playwright. Even if the making of Broadway columns is not quite as corrupt as Odets was to suggest later in *Sweet Smell of Success*, it has always been a chancy affair, with many a slip between PR man and printer. Another Lyons item (Philadelphia *Record*, February 15, 1940), involved Morris Carnovsky and Lee J. Cobb rehearsing for *Night Music;* alas, Cobb was not in that show, but Philip Loeb was and he partnered Carnovsky in the same story when it appeared in the Lyons column in the New York *Post* on

February 2. Which means? Simply, that the night in Sardi's may or may not have taken place and that, if it did, the memory may or may not be fiction. I am prepared to believe that it contains a kind of metaphorical truth, that Odets, by that time busily trying to be a writer, was feeling restricted by the parts he had to play and struggling to break out of them. He must also have known by then that he was not going to expand into leading roles. In any case, if the story is true, Kingsley won. The line about the Boy Scouts is not in the published *Men in White*.

Odets played two roles in Melvin Levy's *Gold Eagle Guy*, which opened on November 28, 1934, and ran until Odets, the playwright, had emerged in public. It was almost his last appearance outside his own work. He did turn up in one of the sketches at a Group benefit at the Civic Repertory Theatre, February 10, 1935 (*Waiting for Lefty* was also on the bill) when he joined J. Edward Bromberg and Walter Coy in "Improvised Operation to the Music of Beethoven." Brooks Atkinson described it as "The most overpowering number. . . . without props, scenery or costumes Mr. Bromberg and two assistants translate their pantomimic surgical operation into a vivid silent drama." When the Group moved *Waiting for Lefty* to Broadway in March of that year, Odets played Dr. Benjamin in the "Interne Episode," leaving the part during the summer for his incredible mission to Cuba. He came back to the show for its last week, and an outraged reviewer in the Brooklyn *Eagle*, convinced that his return was just a box-office trick milking his notoriety, commented on the performance:

> Odets did his brief speaking part with his back to the audience and at that moment was fairly convincing. But for most of the play, as one of the union leaders on the platform . . . Odets was the only one to stare idly about the theater instead of giving attention to the proceedings.

Odets was Dr. Benjamin again, perhaps for sentimental reasons, when the play went to Philadelphia in October of that year, but the Brooklyn *Eagle* reviewer was right. Odets's mind had begun to wander. His acting career had come to an end—unless, of course, we count as acting rather than fun-and-games the brief scene in his first movie, *The General Died at Dawn*, in which he appears as a promoter, trying to sell an oil well to director Lewis Milestone while Hollywood columnist Sidney Skolsky looks on.

Odets had tried for ten years to be an actor, using his minimal skill with little success, but the time had not been wasted. He was still in his twenties when he retired from the boards and he carried with him a strong sense of the performer — his possibilities and his needs — which would serve him as playwright for the rest of his life. George M. Cohan is hardly the performer one would expect to pat a radical playwright on the back, but he praised *Awake and Sing!* in these words: "Full of tricky theatrical touches. It reeks of the theatre, you know." Stanislavsky was making the same point, as a warning, when he told Harold Clurman, "Tell Mr. Odets for me not to give up acting. It will always help him in his playwriting."

Although bad actors have turned into good playwrights in the past (I suspect that Shakespeare is an example), that progression is hardly axiomatic. It took something more than those years of bit parts to make a playwright of Clifford Odets. The strongest influence on him was almost certainly the whole experience of the Group Theatre, and that experience was personal, communal as well as professional. The Group had grown out of the discontent of three young employees of the Theatre Guild—Harold Clurman, Lee Strasberg, Cheryl Crawford—who envisioned a theater as a collective rather than a producing organization, a gathering of individuals, whose plays, artistically and socially, reflected their sense of community, and reached out to touch, to change, to mold the greater society of which both they and their audience were a part. It began with some experimental productions and took clearer shape through hours of talk, weekly meetings which continued from November 1930 to May 1931. That summer, the three directors and a band of actors, moved to the country (Brookfield Center, Connecticut) and began not only to rehearse Paul Green's play for fall production, but to create themselves as a unit, to become both a group and a theater. Clurman's *The Fervent Years* is an account of the ten-year struggle to keep that ideal alive, a story necessarily rife with dissension, desertion, failure. Yet, that first summer (and in fact the first few years) can be characterized—for all the individualistic kicks within the commune—in Clurman's phrase: "Here was companionship, security, work, and dreams."

According to his own testimony, Odets tried to commit suicide three times before he was twenty-five; "once I stopped it myself and twice my life was saved by perfect strangers." On that testimony alone, it is impossible to guess how seriously suicidal Odets was, but the years between Morris High and Brookfield Center could hardly have been as cheerfully difficult as they probably sound in the list of plays and places that mark my account of Odets as actor—particularly to a shy, sensitive young man, somewhat given to masking his distress. "I had made constant references to the boom days of the past," Clurman says in *The Fervent Years,*

> and Clifford Odets wondered what I meant, since in the so-called good times he had virtually been starving, while with the depression the Group had come along and given him hope, enthusiasm, and little but comparatively steady money.

Odets, for all those Philadelphia ties, was looking for a home, and he apparently found it in the Group. He found a community to work in and to live in, both in the summers in the country and in the large flat on West Fifty-seventh Street, where in the leanest days of the early 1930s members of the Group lived and ate together. Within the larger Group, he found a smaller circle of close friends ("my particular chums . . . Elia Kazan, Art Smith, Bud [Roman] Bohnen," he said years later, describing the monumental drunk that followed the optioning of *Awake and Sing!*) and a more formal concentric circle, the Communist Party cell to which he briefly belonged.

In an obituary note in the *Saturday Review,* Clurman recalled that, although Odets was "not a particularly good actor," he seemed to have talent of some undefined kind and, for that reason, he was welcomed into the Group. Although the comment may seem a little too patly after-the-fact, there must have been in the young Odets a quality that did not quite fit the usual theatrical pigeonholes, an unfocused enthusiasm that elicited Stella Adler's "Honestly, Clifford, unless you turn out to be a genius, no one will ever speak to you." Clurman's first impression of Odets, as he describes it in *The Fervent Years*, is of a somewhat peculiar young man with "a tendency to nurse his own oddities," now shyly approaching the girls in the cast, now involved in "raucous philosophical dialogues" with J. Edward Bromberg. "He was given to outbursts of song or sound, forceful but indeterminate as to origin or content." Later, in the winter and spring of 1933, after the debacle of *Big Night*, a difficult time for both Clurman and the Group, the director spent a great deal of time wandering through New York with Odets, letting the younger man introduce him to the poor and the dispossessed, a world foreign to the "enlightened, liberal, and inalterably proper" home Clurman had always known. The Odets peculiarities come across, in the pages describing this hegira, as a sensitivity to people and situations which had not yet found its way to articulacy. Yet, by this time, *Awake and Sing!* was in the making.

It would be a mistake to underestimate what the Group meant to Odets in personal terms or as a setting for the social and political attitudes that he developed during the first years of the 1930s, but there were professional, technical things to be learned too. However small the roles he played, he was at least physically present for most of the early Group productions, on hand to watch the plays take shape in rehearsal. He was also involved, as was the whole troupe, in the exercises that Lee Strasberg developed after having found his way to Stanislavsky through courses with Richard Boleslavsky and Maria Ouspenskaya at the American Laboratory Theater. In an interview with Michael J. Mendelsohn, after commenting on the writers who had affected his work, Odets added, "But my chief influence as a playwright was the Group Theatre acting company, formed and trained and shaped and used by Lee Strasberg." A less explicit testimonial to the Group directors can be found in the early plays, in the affectionate joke of the off-stage names, the Mrs. Strasberg who minds Hennie's baby in *Awake and Sing!* and the Dr. Clurman who looks after Julie in *Paradise Lost*. Long after the Group was gone, Odets still played this name game; Elia Kazan turns up as cucumber seed in *The Flowering Peach*.

CLIFFORD ODETS · *PLAYWRIGHT*

The young Odets also tried his hand at directing. Like a number of the more radical members of the Group, made nervous by the Broadway success of *Men in White*, Odets offered his services to Theatre Union, a united front organization founded to perform leftist plays more professionally than the members of the old League of Workers Theatres could. Molly Day Thacher reported in *New Theatre* that Theatre Union had formed a studio in January 1934 and that Odets, using Stanislavsky-Strasberg methods, was directing scenes from Frederich Wolf's *The Sailors of Catarro*. When Wolf's play finally reached production (December 10, 1934), it was Irving Gordon, not Odets (busy in *Gold Eagle Guy*), who was listed as director, but the family connections were still clear. Mordecai Gorelik, who often designed for the Group, did the sets, and Abner Biberman, part of the old Philadelphia kaffee klatsch, was in the cast. Odets was co-director (with Sanford Meisner) of *Waiting for Lefty*, when it first appeared, but after that, directing, like acting, gave way to writing—at least until the early 1950s when he directed *The Country Girl*, a revival of *Golden Boy* and finally *The Flowering Peach*. By that time he had made his film directorial debut with *None But the Lonely Heart*.

In the discussion of the plays that follows, it will be clear that the ideational treatment of some of Odets's material is a product of his connection with the Group. Never as doctrinairely political as they were sometimes taken to be, the Group did share the leftist optimism of the 1930s and, as *The Fervent Years* indicates, the organization expected its plays to reflect the correct tone of possibility. A group that could persuade Paul Green to substitute an unlikely upbeat ending for the death and disaster with which he originally brought *The House of Connelly* to a close and that could modify the romantic pessimism of Maxwell Anderson in *Night Over Taos* could certainly influence the young Odets enough to insure the hopeful notes with which he ended his plays. "I used to try many ways to make the materials of my plays say something that they really were not saying by tacking on a certain ideological posture," Odets said later. "I think this did damage to the plays and the material, but I couldn't have done otherwise in that period." Of course, it was not simply the Group working on him, but the times that made

31

the Group. Optimism was in the air ("the only thing we have to fear is fear itself").

Perhaps more important than the ideational influence and one that he could have got only from the Group was the structural effect that that organization had on his plays. Odets is one of the few American playwrights who did not fall automatically into the pattern which saw to it that a star part or parts dominated a scene peopled with minor figures. "These early plays were made for the collective acting company technique," Odets said. "They're written for eight characters, with six or seven of the characters of equal importance. Well, this is purely from the Group Theatre ideal of a stage ensemble, and this so fetched me and so took me over that this was how I wrote." Although his figures are not exact, his point is well taken. The special quality of the Odets plays—at least, those written during the 1930s—comes from the fact that he wrote them for particular actors with a definite idea of what a performing company should be, and that he was an active member of that Group when he began to write.

The impulse was older than his association with the Group, as the radio plays mentioned earlier in this chapter indicate. "I always had an ambition to be a writer," he told Burns Mantle. Of his early unproduced plays (the scripts of *Victory* and *910 Eden Street* still exist) he said, in the Mendelsohn interview, "they have no value whatsoever as plays or even scenes." He added:

> They were very painful attempts to . . . find my identity. . . . They also had in them considerable ambition, which simply means a desire to be a playwright, to be a significant writer.

One of the stories that *The Fervent Years* has to tell, a sentence here, a paragraph there, is the slow impingement on Clurman of the seriousness of Odets's desire to be a writer. Describing his response to Odets during that first summer at Brookfield Center, Clurman mentions "an occasional sally into highly charged but vague verbiage in the form of letters and sundry pieces of writing." Shortly after *The House of Connelly* opened, Odets submitted *910 Eden Street* to him:

It dealt with a house in Philadelphia he had lived in, full of confused and unhappy young people. [Odets told John McCarten that it was about "the intelligentsia of Philadelphia."] I hardly thought of it as a play, or of its author as a potential playwright. It was a personal document, such as others brought me from time to time.

The "internal injury," the "pain" that Clurman found in the play is perhaps what Odets was referring to in the Mendelsohn interview when he said that his early works were attempts "to write down the nature of neurotic illness." One of the virtues of *The Fervent Years* is that Clurman is happily aware of his own youthful priggishness, but I am not sure that he recognized how sad and ludicrous the paragraph is in which he tries to recreate his talk with Odets about *910 Eden Street:* a man with an open wound is here being told "to stand up straight and see the world more objectively." Not that the advice is bad for a playwright in embryo.

During the summer of 1932, Odets wrote "a very bad play—about a genius of the Beethoven kind." That was Clurman's judgment and it has not been challenged since. The play is interesting only as a manifestation of Odets's preoccupation with music. Earlier he had written a prose work which he variously described as "a poor novel about a great pianist who lost his left hand in an accident" and "about a young kid violinist who didn't have his violin because the hotel owner had appropriated it for unpaid bills." Perhaps he wrote both. Odets's passion for music was a public love affair. After his first success as a dramatist, interviewers liked to picture him improvising on his Hammond organ ("He cannot play any instrument but likes to strike thundering chords on this organ") or immersing himself in his new record collection. In a letter to Theodore Dreiser, Odets wrote, somewhat ingenuously, "about all I wanted out of life was some certain Beethoven records and I got them with the first play money last year." He said much the same thing to every newspaperman who called him, but he was capable of a grander musical boast: "A good composer was lost when I took up writing." According to Michael J. Mendelsohn, there are notes and diary entries extant which prove "that Odets identified himself closely with Beethoven until his death in 1963." Odets may have been Beethoven at home, but on stage he used everything from Beethoven (Pearl plays "Für Elise" in *Paradise Lost*) to popular songs ("Avalon" finally turned up in *Clash by Night* after not quite making it in the two unproduced plays, *The Silent Partner* and *The Cuban Play*). There is no major work of his in which music does not figure in one way or another, centrally (as in *Golden Boy* and *Night Music*) or peripherally (the radios that have to be turned off in *The Country Girl*), to define character (Jacob in *Awake and Sing!*) or to feed a mood *(None But the Lonely Heart)*. His instruments range from the symphony orchestra *(Humoresque)* to the mythical gitka, the mouse-like creature who sings when Noah's wife dies in *The Flowering Peach*.

There are occasions when Odets's preoccupation with music sits a little grotesquely on his work. The most celebrated example is Gary Cooper's line from *The General Died at Dawn*, "Judy Perrie, darling, we coulda made wonderful music together," a line that, in the variation Murray Kempton gives in *Part of Our Time* ("We could make beautiful music together"), became one of the favorite comic tags of the late thirties. For the most part, however, Odets learned to use music, not to be used by it, and he did so by deserting his beloved Beethoven and coming home to the Bronx. John McCarten quotes a few lines of an Odets diary:

> Here I am writing the Beethoven play, which when it is finished may not even be about Beethoven. Why not write something about the Greenberg family, something I know better, something that is closer to me?

In 1933, he got around to the Greenberg play, although the Greenbergs had become the Bergers, but before *Awake and Sing!* reached the stage, *Waiting for Lefty* had introduced Odets to a small but excited audience.

III. *"already the talk of the town below the Macy-Gimbel line"*

IN THE FALL of 1934, *New Theatre* and *New Masses* announced a jointly sponsored contest, offering fifty dollars for "the best revolutionary play. . . . Any dramatic form," and lesser prizes for shorter, sketch-length plays. The winners were to be announced in the first 1935 issue of both magazines and the three prize plays were to be performed at the Civic Repertory Theatre. When January came, the contest had somehow been forgotten, although both magazines ran advertisements for a New Theatre Night in which *Waiting for Lefty*, "a new revolutionary play by Clifford Odets," was to be presented on a bill with Philip Stevenson's *God's in His Heaven* and the dances of Anna Sokolow. In February, Odets's play, still not wearing a blue ribbon, was published in *New Theatre;* finally in the March issue of that magazine, its editor Herbert Kline (one of the judges) discussed the contest, lamenting the mediocrity of most of the 208 entries and pointing to *Lefty* as the happy exception. Once *Lefty* had been produced, Odets told the House Un-American Activities Committee, "they came to me and said, 'We have had a one-act play contest and no good material has shown up. Do you mind if we give you the prize?'" He did not mind, and so was born the often repeated myth that Odets's first produced play had been written in response to a contest.

Odets's testimony, I suspect, is true, if disingenuous. In disclaiming the contest, he neglects to suggest that there was a motivation beyond the artist's inspiration in the writing of *Lefty*. He had joined the Communist Party toward the end of 1934 and most of the energy of his unit, so Elia Kazan told HUAC, went into "providing 'entertainment' for the meetings and rallies of front organizations and unions." Earlier in 1934, Kazan and Art Smith had written *Dimitroff*, which had been performed at a New Theatre Night on June 3 and published in the July-August number of *New Theatre*. Odets, who had tried unsuccessfully to persuade Smith to help him write *Lefty*, presumably wanted to make a similar contribution, one that at once made a propaganda point and provided a vehicle for amateur production. The League of Workers Theatres° was constantly in search of scripts that its members and other workers' groups might perform in whatever halls were available. Odets has suggested that the impetus for writing *Lefty* was somewhat broader than the CP-New Theatre context: "We thought we ought to have a few of these [one-act plays] in our repertoire for benefit performances." The "we" in this case would seem to be the Group Theatre, and the Group name was often used when members gave their time to special performances. An advertisement *(New Masses,* June 5, 1934) promised a performance of *Dimitroff* by actors from *Men in White* and another *(New Theatre,* January, 1935) said that *Lefty* was to be acted by the "Members of the cast of *Gold Eagle Guy.*"

To win a fifty-buck prize, to serve his party's cause, to stock the Group's benefit bank, simply to try his hand at a propaganda play—for whatever reason or combination of reasons, in the fall of 1934, while the Group was preparing *Gold Eagle Guy*, Odets, by his own admission, wrote *Lefty*, "in three nights in the hotel room in Boston [the Bellevue, according to Elliot Norton] after returning home from the theater about midnight." Perhaps because Lee Strasberg had responded so negatively to the first versions of *Awake and Sing!*, perhaps because his work at the Theatre Union studio had built his directorial confidence, Odets de-

---

°It became the New Theatre League in January 1935, following the pattern of nomenclature shift that its magazine had undergone in September 1933, when *Workers Theatre* was renamed *New Theatre*. It became less narrowly Communist, more United Front at the same time.

cided to stage his own play—or co-stage it, rather, sharing scenes with Sanford Meisner, another of the Group actors. Luther Adler, who played Dr. Benjamin in the early, benefit performances, told Clurman, "Harold, the Group has produced the finest revolutionary playwright in America." Yet, the result was something more than "the most effective agit-prop play written in this country," as Nathaniel Buchwald called *Lefty* in the *Daily Worker.* It burst its bounds, escaped its audience, fed into the mainstream of American drama, dragging its author along.

According to Odets, a "resentful" Strasberg said, "Let 'em fall and break their necks." The imprecation must have worked in the corniest of show business traditions, the bad luck wish ("Break a leg") which, confusing the malevolent gods, brings good luck. The debut was a triumph.

> On Jan. 5, when the curtain rang down on the first performance of Clifford Odets' *Waiting for Lefty* the audience cheered, whistled and screamed with applause. One week later when the same actors had repeated their performances, the Fifth Avenue Theatre, packed to capacity with hundreds of standees, fairly burst with a thunder of hand-claps and shouting.

The description is that of Stanley Burnshaw in *New Masses.* Reminiscences of the first night retain some of the vividness of Burnshaw's on-the-spot report. Harold Clurman, for whom the final, "STRIKE, STRIKE, STRIKE!!!" was "the birth cry of the thirties," wrote in *The Fervent Years:*

> The first scene of *Lefty* had not played two minutes when a shock of delighted recognition struck the audience like a tidal wave. Deep laughter, hot assent, a kind of joyous fervor seemed to sweep the audience toward the stage.

Odets said much the same thing, less forcefully, when he told Michael J. Mendelsohn that "the proscenium arch of the theatre vanished and the audience and the actors were at one with each other," and so did Robert Lewis, one of the original performers, when he described to me how, at the end of the play, the audience and the actors spilled out onto the sidewalk, mingled,

37

moved together—talking, talking, talking,—into a nearby cafeteria, as though this were a magic moment that could not be allowed to die.

Thirty-five years after the fact that initial excitement is a little hard to understand. Although there has been a recent off-Broadway revival of *Waiting for Lefty* (December 13, 1967) and theater became a weapon once again in the 1960s, the naivety, both political and dramatic, of Odets's play is so obvious on the page that one searches for an explanation for all that enthusiasm. Of course, the audience was a special one ("a revolutionary audience," Malcolm Cowley said of a similar occasion, in his speech at the American Writer's Congress, 1935). Certainly the people who came to New Theatre Nights brought their political commitments with them. They must have been analogous to the audiences at religious festivals who, according to T. S. Eliot, "expect to be patiently bored and to satisfy themselves with the feeling that they have done something meritorious." After dutifully chanting "Free *Torgler!* Free *Thaelmann!*" at the end of *Dimitroff*, it must have been overwhelming to get to shout "STRIKE!" having been led to it by the thrust of the play as much as the correctness of the message and by characters who were not simply slogans, who had at least a family resemblance to one's fellow human beings. Even in 1935, there were critics—some (Burnshaw, for instance) admirers of the play—who could catalog its faults, but their voices were almost lost in the chorus of celebration.

After the initial reception of *Lefty,* it turned up on one benefit bill after another—once (March 3) appropriately enough, for the taxi drivers. Sometimes it appeared with the Stevenson play, sometimes with *Dimitroff,* sometimes with the Group sketches, but Odets's play was the thing to see. By the time *Awake and Sing!* opened, Robert Garland could describe Odets as "already the talk of the town below the Macy-Gimbel line." And above it, too, for most of the reviewers had already seen *Lefty* by this time and *Stage* even carried a rumor that Lee Shubert wanted to bring the show uptown. (That *Stage* article incidentally contains the most restrained description ever written of the end of *Lefty:* "The last line—'Shall we strike?'—brought the audience to its feet as one man with a shout of 'Yes!' ") It was the Group, not Lee Shubert, that brought *Lefty* to Broadway, on a double bill with a new Odets one-acter, *Till the Day I Die,* written for the occasion. It opened at the Longacre on March 26, 1935 to generally favorable reviews; and, after 136 performances, with the closing of *Day,* it moved to the Belasco and ran for a week with *Awake and Sing!* In the fall, while the Group was readying its new plays, *Lefty* and *Awake* reopened (September 9) for a three-week run and then moved on to Philadelphia where they played five weeks.

The active life of *Waiting for Lefty,* the one for which it was created, did not depend on Broadway. The play went immediately into production all over the country—amateur production, more often than not, sponsored by workers' groups. According to Albert Maltz, by July 1935, it had played in thirty cities; a few months later Odets would exclaim in *New Theatre,* "*Waiting for Lefty* plays in 104 American cities in eight months!" Part of the play's attraction lay with the enemies it made. The attacks on *Lefty* during 1935 were so strenuous that Elmer Davis, speaking for the Authors' League of America, accused municipalities of using "fire laws, obsolete statutes from the old 'blue laws' period, red tape in connection with licenses" to attack "freedom of opinion." In Richard Pack's "The Censors See Red!" the lion's share of the horrible examples fall to *Lefty.* Three may stand for many. In Boston, when the owner of the Long Wharf was warned that he was housing "communistic groups," he evicted the New Theatre Players. When the production was moved to the Dudley Street Opera House, the police arrested the cast "on a charge of using profanity in a public assembly." In Newark, when the Collective Theatre finally found a hall (their third try), the police broke up the production and arrested nine people; later the play was done in Newark, because, so Burns Mantle reports, an "earnest young woman" persuaded the New York drama editors to quiet the Newark police. In New Haven, the school board revoked the permission they had given, declaring the play "unfit to be produced in a public school building," but the protests of the Yale faculty and students won the day and the Unity Players, which had just received the Baker Cup at Yale for their *Lefty,* went on with their production. Long after the censorship furor died down, *Lefty* remained a favorite with the small socially oriented drama groups; probably only Irwin Shaw's *Bury the Dead* (1936) rivaled it in popularity. A list of the bookings of the Detroit Contemporary Theatre in *New Theatre News* (December, 1938) shows that *Lefty* was the play most often offered to the unions for whom the company played. A New York *Times* story on the London opening of *Awake and Sing!* in 1938 made the point that " 'Waiting for Lefty' long has been firmly established as the most considerable work in the repertory of the British workers' drama groups." There was even the accolade of parody; the best known take-off was *Waiting for Odets,* which the Chicago Repertory Group put together in 1935 and was still doing in 1940. Odets's play was almost an institution.

When *Waiting for Lefty* was published in *New Theatre* it carried the subtitle, "A Play in Six Scenes, Based on the New York City Taxi Strike of February, 1934." It has been customary in general comments on the play to repeat the easy label, one that gives a suggestion of historicity without the need to be specific. The 1934 taxi strike however, was a somewhat complicated one, likely to place Odets's play in an oblique light.

It began on February 2 in a quarrel over the dispensation of a five-cent fare tax which had been declared unconstitutional. Fiorello LaGuardia, then mayor, had suggested that the five-cent charge remain and be given to the drivers whose tips had dropped after the tax was put on; the companies suggested a 60-40 split in their favor. Within the week (February 8), the drivers settled at 50-50, but the strike was far from over. The taxi men had no organization when they went out but from the strike itself emerged the Taxi Drivers Union of Greater New York, a confederation of drivers' groups from the various boroughs. A second demand, for the recognition of the union, was not granted in the first settlement. It was this demand that triggered the second strike, March 10, although the ostensible cause was the firing of a driver by the Parmelee System.

By this time, there was a fight within the TDU between the men who had run the February strike and the new leaders, of which Samuel Orner, head of the Manhattan union, and the organizer, Joseph Gilbert, were the most important. Burnshaw's review of *Lefty* reports that, at the second performance, Gilbert stepped from the wings "to say that just such a meeting as Odets presents took place last March when the members of the Union met in the Bronx and overwhelmingly voted to strike." Not that Sam and Joe, as they were called in *New Masses* (line drawings of them accompany Joseph North's "Taxi Strike" in the April 3 issue), ever had the full support that a theatre "STRIKE" cry implies. For the moment dominant, they called a general strike on March 17, but it was not nearly so effective as the February strike had been. The situation was further complicated by the formation of a Parmelee company union (headed by "Mr. Irving 'Rat' Robbins," as North called him) and, as the trouble spread, similar organizations in the other companies. Violence began, according to the New York *Times,* when one thousand striking drivers marched through midtown, wrecking cabs that were still in service.° While LaGuardia's office and the Regional Labor Board tried to work out a plebiscite on union representation (which no one—the companies, their house unions, the TDU—seemed to want), the violence continued.

There were charges of gangsterism on both sides. LaGuardia warned the strikers that there were gangsters among them and implied that the companies were using "Chicago strong-arm men." Orner had earlier denied that he was using "guerillas": "The drivers are pretty good with their fists and know how to use them, I have found. We don't need any gangster to help us." North, celebrating the ingenuity of the striking hackies, described "the Education Committee . . . which is a guerilla picket line well adapted to the needs of a big city strike of this sort . . . the scab finds his car doorless or even in flames." One of North's hackies said that the scabbing taxis were driven by "Chicago gunmen wit' soft hats," and there was apparently

---

°Albert Halper's "Scab!" is a short story about a cabbie who spends the day avoiding punishing strikers, piling up an impressive eleven dollars to take home to his sick wife and children. "It was the most I had ever made in a single day's hacking." In the end, he succumbs to guilt, smashes the windows and dents the fenders of his own cab and vows to scab no more. The story was published in *American Mercury,* June 1934.

some truth to the charge. In *I Break Strikes!*,* Edward Levinson
mentions casually, as though everyone knew, that Max Sherwood's Eagle Industrial Associates—one of whose hoods was
called Taxi Murray—helped break the 1934 taxi strike.

The taxi strike was broken. The TDU accepted defeat. Orner
tried to put a brave mouth on it, promising a stronger union to
come, but he and Gilbert, among others, were expelled from
TDU, accused of "conducting the strike for the benefit of the
Communist party, rather than for the union membership and of
having caused the loss of the strike by this action." This thumb-
nail history of the taxi strike indicates the distance between the
simple, black-and-white world of the propaganda play and the
gray reality which it presumably reflects and certainly serves.

In answer to a direct question at the HUAC hearing about
whether *Lefty* had been based on the strike, Odets answered,
"That is what they** say. But it is just something I kind of made
up. . . . I didn't know anything about a taxicab strike. . . . I
have never been near a strike in my life." In an oblique way
what he is saying is probably true, even though, when *Lefty* was
new, he was quoted in the *Daily Worker*, "The play was written
out of admiration for the boys who fought along with Joe Gilbert and Sam Orner against LaGuardia's cops and the
taxi-company's scabs." I suspect that it was not the strike, but
Joseph North's article on it, which gave rise to the play; Odets's
direct borrowing, minimal as it is, suggests that. North uses,
almost as an epigraph, a long paragraph identified as "Hackie's
Fable," in which the wife demands—as Edna does in the first
scene of *Lefty*—that the driver choose between her and the
company. Agate's identification of the Communist salute with
the "good old uppercut to the chin" at the end of Odets's play
comes directly from North ("His left fist—a huge affair—goes up

*Levinson's book is primarily about the techniques of Pearl L. Bergoff,
self-styled "King of the Strikebreakers." The line in *Lefty* about "that Bergman
outfit on Columbus Circle" is probably a half-remembered reference to Bergoff,
who once had offices at 2 Columbus Circle and who would certainly have been
one of the villains in any Leftist strikelore.
**This is presumably the same *they* who appears in the contest disavowal I
quoted earlier. Odets's use of the pronoun in his testimony suggests a disengaging
otherness.

in a sort of short uppercut"), although North goes Odets one better at the tough metaphor game by letting his Pondsie call it "The left hook." Of course, Odets may not have been aware of his debt to North by the time he put words on paper. All of his plays are full of echoes—quotations, songs, taglines, sometimes identified, sometimes not—which suggest that his was a kind of flypaper talent, pulling ideas and phrases out of the air. That I recognize "Come out in the light, Comrade," the line that ends the actor's scene, as a variation on the Black Man's "Come into the light, comrades, come into the light" from *Newsboy,* the play that Gregory Novikov made from a V. J. Jerome poem, does not mean that Odets consciously used *Newsboy,* even though (since the Workers Laboratory Theatre was acting it in 1934 and Jerome was a kind of cultural commissar for the Party) he probably knew the play. Even if Odets had used this material deliberately—patting a bit of North into place here, a touch of Jerome there, a whisper of Alfred Kreymborg (I think I hear echoes of the "Poor couple" scene from *America, America!* in the Joe-Edna quarrel) elsewhere—it would have been perfectly legitimate; in the context in which art is a weapon rather than an individual investment, this is not literary cannibalism but the proper use of existing tools.

Waiting for Lefty says a great deal less about the actual taxi strike of 1934 than it does, by implication, about the general labor situation of the time. The assumption, on the Left, was that the working man was being victimized not only by his employer but by a combination of politicians (headed by President Roosevelt) and dishonest labor leaders (the AFL as a gigantic company union). "We suppose that the supporters of the New Deal will admit that its purpose is to save American capitalism" (*New Masses,* March 1934). The NRA was seen as a first step toward fascism and the reigning assumption (as in Sid's big speech in *Lefty*) was that there was always a capitalistic war ready to chew up the workers when they were no longer usable on the production line. The cover of *New Masses* for August 1933 shows the NRA Eagle with a worker crushed in one claw, guns in the other; a good strong working-class arm is reaching onto the page, wringing the bird's neck: WE DO OUR PART. The network of villains might not be quite so wide outside the

Communist press; but, at a time when militant unionism was pushing into new industries, upsetting not only the companies but the old labor status quo, its sympathizers—as the labor reporting in *Nation* and *New Republic* shows—shared the same general frame of reference. For this reason, Odets is able to use simple indicators, knowing that his audience will respond as he himself does to "textile strike" or "the man in the White House."

His Harry Fatt is conceived as the most obvious kind of corrupt union leader; his description ("A fat man of porcine appearance") leans heavily on the standard cartoon stereotype. If this were not immediately clear when the audience saw him (Russell Collins, who played Fatt originally, does not fit the description at all), it would be apparent as soon as he begins to speak, trying to persuade his own union that this is not the time to strike. "Look at the textile strike—out like lions and in like lambs." The textile strike had ended in September 1934 with none of its demands granted, and Frank Gorman, the AFL strike leader who had refused left-wing aid, was already becoming the villain in what the *New Masses* called the "super-super-super strike sell-out." "Take the San Francisco tie-up—starvation and broken heads." This is a reference to the maritime strike, but attitudes toward it can be seen in *Nation's* report on the three-day sympathy general strike which took place when "patriotic A.F. of L. members . . . stirred by the fiery appeals of Harry Bridges and other ardent strike-leaders of the I.L.A., bolted from the control of their usual masters, the reactionary labor leaders." "The steel boys wanted to walk out, too, but they changed their minds." In "The Steel Strike Collapses," Louis Adamic explained that the conservative labor leaders, in order to forestall the Communists and the radicals, started an organization drive of their own and held out a possibility of action, only to take shelter in William Green's call for mediation and to kill the expected strike. In each of these lines, Fatt says, look, strikes fail, and the audience hears, corrupt leaders sell out the workers. So, too, with the rest of his speech. Fatt's reference to Roosevelt ("looking out for our interests") suggests the remark of "one of the dubious leaders of the taxi men" whom Joseph North quotes: "that Great Humanitarian in

Washington who won't let us suffer injustice." When Fatt calls a heckler "you damn red," the audience recognizes it as a too familiar tactic. "Our officials yelled 'Reds' at us, just like the police," complained a mill worker in still another *New Masses* article on the textile strike. Fatt's catalog of Russian crimes—endangering both Christ and virtuous woman-hood—could have come directly from the Hearst papers; as Ferdinand Lundberg indicates in *Imperial Hearst,* the pub-lisher initiated a particularly strong anti-communist campaign in late 1934.

In Fatt's first speech and throughout the play, Odets pulls his references out of the recent headlines (as he often does in later plays), but their use in *Waiting for Lefty* depends on a particu-lar response rather than simple recognition. Given this pattern, it is surprising that more people did not call him out on the strike about which he was ostensibly writing. Some reviewers, like Percy Hammond of the *Herald Tribune* and Richard Lock-ridge of the *Sun,* did consult a taxi driver or two, convincing themselves that Odet's figures ("six-seven dollars a week") were wrong,* but it took Bill Shulman on the *Socialist Call* to ques-tion "the facts . . . since as history bears out, the leaders them-selves were communists, who called the strike prematurely." Odets's crowd would presumably answer that it was not bad tactics, but a combination of liberal politics, big business and labor stooging that broke the strike. Shulman, of course, did not speak out of simple objectivity. His and other Socialist reviews displayed an understandable distrust of the Communists, since it was only recently (a *New Masses* drama review on November 27, 1934 praised a "First United Front" event) that the Commu-nists had decided that maybe, after all, the Socialists were not their chief class enemy. Joseph T. Shipley in the *New Leader* added this qualification to his praise of *Lefty:* "It is guilty of the frequent Communist playing into Fascist hands, in its picture of the labor leader as a capitalist rat." The *New Leader*—compared to the *Call*—was a conservative Socialist voice, and it was in its pages that the oddest political response to *Lefty* appeared. Ger-trude Weil Klein, deprecating "the wild acclaim of the

* An NRA report quoted in the New York *Times,* March 13, 1934, suggests that Odets was not far off.

self-appointed Bolshevik interpreters of the working class," attacked the play and did so by dipping into reminiscence, recalling or inventing a "Cliff Odets" who used to hang around Greenwich Village and to whom she attributed the remark, "The workers stink." The protests were so immediate and so loud (from Odets, the Group, *New Theatre*) that the *New Leader* printed an apology although, as the *Daily Worker* pettishly said, it was in "an inconspicuous corner." The Socialists were having internecine trouble of their own at this time, a split between the Militants, who wanted to work with the Communists, and the old-line Socialists. Given that situation, the Odets character who says, "The MILITANT! Come out in the light, Comrade," might appear to be doing something more than attempting to awaken the apolitical actor, might seem to be meddling in a private quarrel. Since none of the Socialist reviewers mentioned this point and since Odets was not the kind of theoretical Communist who played the hair-splitting ideational games so popular in the early 1930s, the use of MILITANT to balance "the meek" may be no more than one of the echoes I talked about earlier.

It was, of course, only in the leftist press that Odets's play got the kind of attention a propaganda play might be expected to elicit. Whether the uptown reviewers responded for or against the play politically, it was a reaction to the generalized radical thrust of the play rather than to the specific nuances. Once the play got to Broadway, the audiences—even though they were generally sympathetic to the play's message—could hardly have been as sensitive to the implications of "San Francisco" or "steel boys" as the special audiences for which it was presumably written. As the decade wore on and *Lefty* remained a favorite for amateur production, the references certainly lost their immediate meaning as well as their emotional freight. *Waiting for Lefty* was obviously created by the political-labor-theatrical context of 1934, but it was also created by a playwright, which may explain why it turned out to be so much hardier than the others of its breed—all as ephemeral as the daily paper. It had (perhaps still has) a dramatic vitality that can be understood only by taking a close look at how it was put together.

In the "Notes for Production" originally published with *Wait-*

ing for Lefty, Odets said, "The form used is the old black-face minstrel form of chorus, end men, specialty men and interlocutor." More than twenty-five years later, he was still insisting that the minstrel show was his structural source, although he admitted that the play "took its form necessarily from what we then called the agit-prop form." Except for the fact that a circle of performers sits on stage and that now one, now another steps out of that circle to do an act of his own, the minstrel analogy is very tenuous. *Lefty* is more obviously an agitprop. Ben Blake, in his pamphlet *The Awakening of the American Theatre* (1935), explained that agitprop became popular with workers' theaters around New York in the early 1930s. The Prolet-Buehne, a German-speaking group, introduced the form as early as 1928, and the Workers Laboratory Theatre (founded in 1930) developed a similar kind of program on its own; eventually the two groups made contact and by the time the first National Workers Theatre Conference was held in 1932, the agitprop was the accepted dramatic weapon. Blake, thinking of the Prolet-Buehne's *Scottsboro,* called the agitprop "a new, chanted type of play," but the unsigned preface to the drama section of *Proletarian Literature in the United States* (a collection that Granville Hicks, *et al.* put together in 1935 for International Publishers) differentiated between works like *Scottsboro* ("This was the mass chant, consisting of a simple factual story, or a poem, which builds to a direct agitational appeal") and another kind of short play "written generally in doggerel, with stylized characters representing the boss, the worker, the militarist, the imperialist nations . . . really an animated cartoon, with a specific political message, delivered in schematic form." Perhaps the two can be seen as representing the two sides of the generic name (agitation and propaganda), but the forms (like the name) never remained separate; chants and cartoons alike had a way of pulling the audience, verbally at least, into the action. The function of the agitprop, after all, was to manipulate the audience, to elicit a particular response, one that hopefully would persist after the audience left the theater. A report on that first national conference outlined one of the basic tasks of the workers' theater: "to arouse the workers for the defense of the Soviet Union, against the coming imperialist attack." The issue of *Workers*

47

Theatre for June-July, 1932, contained a typical collection of early agitprops that illustrate both the crudity of the form and the implementation of the task quoted above. *15 Minute Red Revue,* by John E. Bonn of the Prolet-Buehne, ends with its eleven performers asking, in unison, "Where is your future?" and then crying out, presumably joined by the audience, "FOR THE SOVIET UNION!!!" Both the anonymous *Vote Communist* ("An Election Play for Street Performances") and Nathaniel Buchwald's *Hands Off!* ("An Election Agitprop Play for Indoor Performances," translated from the Yiddish of J. Shapiro) end with the cry "VOTE COMMUNIST!" A sophistication of the form can be seen in the Smith-Kazan *Dimitroff* ("A Play of Mass Pressure"). Bad as it is, it is far superior to something like *Hands Off!* It builds to the usual audience chant, but it does so by using brief scenes—sometimes slapstick, sometimes serious—that give a cartoon account of the burning of the Reichstag and the subsequent attempt to place the blame on the Communists.

Odets may not have known the 1932 agitprops mentioned above, but he was certainly familiar with *Dimitroff*. He may even have acted in it. *Waiting for Lefty* is, of course, a great advance over the Smith-Kazan play, but the influence of *Dimitroff* and the agitprop in general can be plainly seen—in the characters, the ending and the relationship between performers and audience. Joseph Wood Krutch's complaint, "The villains are mere caricatures and even the very human heroes occasionally freeze into stained-glass attitudes," is an accurate criticism. Yet it is misleading because it assumes that Odets is mainly concerned with psychological depth, which is not the case. His characters are not thin realistic figures but thickened out agit-prop cartoons. This can be seen in his use of significant names: what are "Fatt" and "Lefty" but labels?° The primary function of the scenes, for all the praise they received, was pedagogical; each had a point to make (the same point: the situation is unbearable, refuse to bear it) and, within the total context of the

°This use of names—which was also a way of working out character traits for Odets, as Lewis Milestone's article in the October 1936 *Stage* indicates—remained a favorite device for the playwright, even after he began to work in a more conventional realistic form. From Mr. Carp in *Golden Boy* to the ironic Buddy Bliss in *The Big Knife*, Odets continued to use names as indicators.

play, that point is more important than the incidental pleasures of character and dramatic action.

As for the ending, Lefty's "STRIKE, STRIKE, STRIKE!!!" is obviously one with the cries that brought the other agitprops to a close. In one sense only. Ideally the manipulation in agitprops is both artistic and political. The final cry is the inevitable result of the play itself, but it, in turn, is a new beginning. One not only shouted "VOTE COMMUNIST!," one presumably went out and did so. One not only shouted, "Free *Torgler!* Free *Thaelmann!,*" one did what one could about it; an introductory note to *Dimitroff* said, "It should lead directly into the present mass-struggle to force the release of Thaelmann and Torgler." One not only shouted, "STRIKE, STRIKE, STRIKE!!!" but . . . what? The taxi strike was over; no new one was being planned; even if it were, the audience—except perhaps on the night of the taxi driver's benefit—would not directly be involved. We can assume, as Frederick A. Pottle did when he reviewed the published play, that the final shouts "refer to no mere cab-drivers' revolt," that the play ends "in a lyric proclamation of the proletarian revolution." In fact, we should so assume. *Lefty* is a call to action, but the action is amorphous, the revolution is metaphorical. The direct line between play and political action breaks down. The final STRIKE cry is a cousin to Aristotelian catharsis, a fulfilling of the audience, a moment of community that substitutes for direct action and makes it unnecessary. *Lefty* fails as agitprop because it succeeds too obviously as a play.

The last shout is only the most overt example of the way *Lefty* breaks down the conventional separation of audience and performers. The audience has a role to play from the beginning. It is the union meeting, being harangued from the stage, and there are plants in the auditorium—hecklers, the man who runs on stage in the "Labor Spy Episode"—to help give the whole thing verisimilitude. Helen Deutsch, in charge of publicity for the Group, explained in the New York *Herald Tribune* that the production used only five actors in the audience "but occasionally they seem like twenty, because so many persons are seeing the play for the second or even third time that they know all the answers, and lift their voices to help response." For John Mason Brown this was "an old Reinhardt trick," and a number of reviewers invoked Pirandello. Miss Deutsch herself pointed out that audience plants had been used in the Theatre Union production of *Peace on Earth* by George Sklar and Albert Maltz, and in John Galsworthy's *The Skin Game*. Since the nonrealistic staging of *Peace on Earth* was abandoned in rehearsal (so Morgan Y. Himelstein says in *Drama Was A Weapon*, and the reviews seem to bear him out) and the Galsworthy play, which did plant bidders in the audience in the auction scene, had been performed in 1920, when Odets was still a schoolboy, I like to think Miss Deutsch was joking. In fact, she was probably simply doing her PR job, helping to keep *Lefty* on the drama pages, but her examples might be a way of saying *what is all this nonsense about Pirandello*. *Lefty* is a revolutionary play, but Odets was certainly not involved in an aesthetic revolution. Aside from *The Cuban Play*, which was never produced, *Lefty* is the only play in which Odets abandoned the conventional realistic form. He did so, however, without abandoning convention. The play does not destroy the proscenium arch because, in its proper setting, there would be no proscenium arch. *Lefty* was written to be performed by small groups, in union halls, schoolrooms, anywhere. It was only chance—a play that good emerging at a time so congenial to propaganda—that it ended up on the stage of the Longacre Theatre, looking like one of Pirandello's progeny. In its use of the audience—much more than its characters, which keep slipping out of their cartoon origins, or its ending, in which agitation is infected with art—*Lefty* is most obviously an agitprop.

The central action of *Waiting for Lefty* is not the waiting itself but the struggle that takes place for control of the union meeting. As the play opens Harry Fatt—with his gunman lolling down left, making an occasional threatening gesture—appears to be in control of the situation. Although his opening speech is designed (by Odets) to turn the audience against him, he is so sure of himself that he can taunt the members of the committee, can even indulge them: "Sure, let him talk." Joe's speech turns into his scene with Edna, but the audience has never left the union hall. "The seated men are very dimly visible in the outer dark," the stage direction says, "but more prominent is Fatt smoking his cigar and often blowing the smoke in the lighted circle." There is a photograph of the original production which indicates very clearly how the flashbacks are made to exist both in the past that they are remembering and in the present of the meeting. Ruth Nelson (as Edna) can be seen in her own shaft of light, but the committee is more than "dimly visible;" a light behind has turned the sitting figures into silhouettes, unmistakably if inactively part of her scene. The meeting once again takes center stage in Episode IV when Fatt introduces "Tom Clayton from little ole Philly" to warn them against going out on strike. There had been a taxicab strike in Philadelphia, a bloody one, at the beginning of 1934, but, unlike the New York strike, it ended with the recognition of the union. Although knowledge of that successful strike adds an irony to Clayton's appearance, the scene is much more conventional than that subtlety suggests. The unmasking of the spy was practically mandatory in a labor play; *Peace on Earth*, which Odets would have known, had such a scene in 1933, but it was a standard before that (see *Gods of the Lightning*, the 1928 play by Maxwell Anderson and Harold Hickerson). Odets's variation (perhaps an unconscious throwback to all those Civil War stories in which brother met brother on the battlefield) lets the spy's brother expose him. If the play were taken as unbendingly realistic, one would have to assume that Clayton was on the agenda before the meeting began, that Fatt intended to use him in any case, but Odets's realism is only as real as the immediate dramatic demand allows it to be. Fatt obviously introduces Clayton at this point because he senses that the meeting is slipping away from him and Odets lets him do so to remind the audience, who has presumably been moved by the first three scenes, that the struggle is not over yet. At this point, it might be a good idea to look at those scenes.

The two most successful episodes, as miniature plays, are the first ("Joe and Edna") and the third ("The Young Hack and His Girl"). Both are domestic scenes. The former is simply a family quarrel which follows a familiar pattern. The wife, unable to persuade her husband with words, threatens to leave him, and thereby wins the argument; such a scene traditionally ends with an embrace and so does this one—although it is Joe's embrace of the cause. The other is a lovers-parting play, poured into the Depression mold. Although Irv warns his sister that she must give up Sid, it is economic conditions, not the family, that come between them. This situation—the impossibility of marriage in a world where poverty turns love sour (see Edna's "Do it in the movies, Joe—they pay Clark Gable big money for it," when she refuses to let him touch her in Episode I)—is one of the reigning clichés of the 1930s. Group audiences already knew it from the Siftons' *1931*—. It is based on the very real fact that marriages fell off when the Depression was at its worst. By the time Odets got around to using it, however, it was less a reflection of fact (there were more marriages in 1934 than in 1929) than a sentimental indicator of a world out of joint. It was a favorite with Odets. It recurs in *Awake and Sing!* and *Paradise Lost* and—long after it seems appropriate—in *Night Music* and *Clash by Night.* That Odets was aware that it was a variation on an ancient dramatic situation can be seen from his first use of it in *I Got the Blues,* the early version of *Awake and Sing!;* there, as though he were unsure that it was enough to let the economy come down on the shoulders of Ralph and his girl, he made her a Catholic and let Bessie worry about her being a *shikse* as well as a poor orphan. The economic situation may be the ultimate subject of Episode III, but its dramatic heart is the farewell itself. Sid and Florrie play at being movie lovers, a game that collapses under their distress. Unlike Adam and his girl in *1931*—, whose farewell scene follows their making love, Sid and Florrie remain pure (he gallantly refuses her offer), an instance in which Odets's romanticism becomes a device that lets his two characters remain vulnerable children. Since both these scenes follow standard patterns, their distinctive quality lies in the characters and their language, the way in which they use words connotatively (Edna's "Get out of here!" means "I love you") and jokes as protective devices (Florrie answers Sid's "What's on your mind?" with "The French and Indian War").

At first glance the second scene, "Lab Assistant Episode," might seem out of place between these other two. It introduces the first of the middle-class characters, about whom John Howard Lawson said, "One cannot reasonably call these people 'stormbirds of the working class.'" It does not dramatize the conditions which are pushing the taxi drivers to strike as the two domestic scenes do; instead, it shows the moment in which

Miller loses his job and, thus, explains how he came to drive a taxi. In that way, it resembles the fifth and sixth episodes, which may be the reason the scene was dropped when the play was printed in *New Theatre* and *Proletarian Literature in the United States*. Yet, Episode II belongs with the first group because it, too, is a standard dramatic situation. The propaganda content of the scene, the pacifism that looked back to World War I (Miller's lines about his dead brother) and forward to the next war ("The world is an armed camp today"), masks a simple worm-turns situation. Clean-living Miller (he neither drinks nor smokes), conventionally subservient to those above him, finds himself, line by line, acceding to Fayette on matters about which he really does not agree (that the victims of World War I "died in a good cause," that the making of poison gas is necessary); he finally reaches his breaking point when Fayette asks him to spy on his superior. A good American boy, conditioned not to snitch on his buddies, his sense of honor forces the whole industrial structure into a new perspective, and, like the doting schoolboy who discovers that the basketball star is a bully not a hero, Miller hits Fayette in the mouth. "Fatt, of course, represents the capitalist system throughout the play," Odets says in the "Notes," and although the text does not specifically call for doubling—as it does later with the producer in Episode V—Russell Collins played Fayette as well as Fatt in the original Broadway production. The audience, recognizing Fatt in Fayette, will not, then, be watching the scene to see *what* will happen; it is the *when* that holds them, and the punch in the mouth is the fulfillment of audience expectations.

Although the three episodes contain direct propaganda statements, particularly in the speeches of Edna and Sid, the scenes are designed to work conventionally, to elicit audience sympathy, thus unloosening Fatt's hold on the meeting. Hence, his need for Clayton in Episode IV. After the failure of that ruse, the next speakers attack more directly, the scenes—"The Young Actor" and "Interne Episode"—become more sermons than dramatic scenes. It is true that Episode V is a comic turn of sorts in the caricature of the producer as businessman and there is a whisper of plot in the humiliation and rejection of the actor, but the main thrust of the scene lies in the exhortations of the secretary, her giving the actor a copy of *The Communist Manifesto* and inviting him to come into the light. The scene was dropped when *Lefty* was reprinted in *Six Plays* because it was "too untypical," a product of the immediate professional concerns of Odets and his fellow actors; or so Odets told Mendelsohn. I can think of at least one other reason why it might have been pulled. It is the most unequivocal statement of the play's Communist position. Even Agate's speech at the end works in metaphor (the uppercut) and allusion ("STORMBIRDS OF THE WORKING-CLASS"). If this is a correct guess, it is not simply a matter of the Odets of 1939 withdrawing a little from the Odets of 1935. The cast list suggests that the actor's scene had disappeared from *Lefty* by September 1935, when the play reopened on Broadway. In that case, it may be a matter of Odets, the Broadway playwright, withdrawing a little from Odets, the Communist playwright.

Episode VI, which today might be called a spin-off of *Men in White*, is a simple revelation scene, in which Dr. Benjamin learns that he is being fired because he is a Jew and the two doctors learn that the charity patient has died at the hands of an incompetent but well-connected intern. The meat of the scene is in the speeches of Dr. Barnes, who is old and corrupted by society, and can only ask Benjamin to act for him ("When you fire the first shot say, 'This one's for old Doc Barnes!' "); and in Benjamin's decision not to run to Russia but to stay and "Fight! Maybe get killed, but goddam! We'll go ahead!"

When we return to the meeting at the end of the play to hear Agate's speech, to learn that Lefty is dead, to answer the call to strike, we find that the previous two scenes have completely routed Fatt. He and his gunman are reduced to a show of violence, and even that is ineffective as the committee members step between them and Agate. Lawson, criticizing the development of *Lefty* as a play, says that the emotional intensity comes not from the action but from "the increasingly explicit statement of revolutionary protest," but he is working out of a too conventional idea of drama. Surely the growing explicitness is the motivational force in the action, the persuasive power that lets the committee convince themselves and finally the meeting (the audience) that the power in the hall (the theater? the country?) must pass to them. Lawson calls the play "a study in conversions," and, indeed, the scenes do detail past conversions (I, II, V, VI) or the situation out of which conversion will come (III); but these scenes become converting mechanisms themselves, turning the committeemen from simply followers of Lefty to active strike leaders. That is why the news of Lefty's death is introduced at the end, almost an afterthought; it is the immediate trigger to the strike call, but it is not an important motivating event in the creation of a climate in which the cry of "STRIKE!" becomes possible. Lefty's absence provides an occasion, but his death is only an emotional fillip; the play has already reached its conclusion when the committeemen stop Fatt's attack on Agate. All that remains is for the audience to ratify that fact which—this being an agitprop—they do not by applauding, but by shouting "STRIKE!"

Today *Waiting for Lefty* is considered little more than an historical artifact, and so it is. Yet its position as a representative propaganda play of the period rests in great part on the fact that, for all the crudities inherent in the form, it is an impressively made play, tailored to do a specific job. It is also the play in which the Odetsian style first burst on an unsuspecting public, but I prefer to consider that style in the next chapter, the discussion of *Awake and Sing!* which—despite the accident of production—is really Odets's first play and his best.

IV. *"I wouldn't trade you for two pitchers and an outfielder"*

U NDERSTAND THAT I'm supposed to confess how I came to write 'Awake and Sing!'" Odets wrote in the New York *World-Telegram*. "I was sore; that's why I wrote that play. I was sore at my whole life. [cf. Kewpie's "I'm sore on my whole damn life," in *Paradise Lost*.] Getting nothing done. Stuffed in a room waiting for Luther Adler to perish so I might get a chance at playing his part in 'Success Story.'" Adler never missed a performance.

It was the unhappy winter of 1932-33. Odets was living in the community apartment which the most indigent members of the company shared ("the Group's poorhouse," Harold Clurman called it in *The Fervent Years*), and it was there—"stuffed" in the smallest room, sitting on a camp bed, his typewriter on his knees—that he wrote the first two acts of *I Got the Blues*. Whether the third was finished in Lee Strasberg's "kitchen, on the bread board," as Odets said in the article quoted above, or in his parents' house in Philadelphia, as he later recalled, a first version of the play was ready by the summer of 1933 when the Group left for Green Mansions (an adult camp in Warrensburg, New York) to begin rehearsals of *Men in White*.

Awake and Sing!, in this embryonic form, was first performed at Green Mansions. The deal was that the Group, in exchange for a place to live and work, would provide entertainment—

plays, sketches, songs—for the camp. One of their programs was a try-out production of the second act of *I Got the Blues*. "To our surprise and delight," Clurman later recalled in the New York *Herald Tribune*, (March 10, 1935) "the audiences chuckled, guffawed and even roared nearly all the way through." Since this line was written while *Awake* was on Broadway, when it would have been useful to remind potential theatergoers that Odets's play is a mixture of "Joy and Sadness," as the headline had it, one might suspect a little overstatement. Still, it is a publicity reflection of the truth, for Clurman reported in *The Fervent Years* that "the audience loved it." Yet, the Group, to Odets's chagrin, did nothing about it, probably, as Clurman admitted, because even so happy a reception could not erase his first reaction to the script: "The first act was cluttered with some rather gross Jewish humor and a kind of messy kitchen realism; the last act I thought almost masochistically pessimistic." Certainly *Blues* is heavily larded with Yiddish phrases, most of which disappear in *Awake* ("An 'aus-ga-shlept' dish rag" becomes "A little dope"), if that is what Clurman meant by "gross Jewish humor," but I suspect that the real complaint was that the original mother is much more cruel than the Bessie of *Awake* and the ending of *Blues* has hardly a glimmer of hope. Clurman had never been happy with Odets's "peculiar sense of gloomy fatality," as he called it in *The Fervent Years*, and a very black *Blues* must have upset the Group's "own sense of the perfectability of man" in 1933, as much as the original violent ending of *The House of Connelly* had in 1931. Like Uncle Morty in *Awake*, offering Hennie a couple of dresses from the "eleven-eighty" line, the Group was willing to give Odets encouragement, "Only don't sing me the blues."

The play was to have a *Wanderjahr* in the land of might-have-been before it finally came home again to a Group ready to receive it. According to Odets, it was Louis Simon, a fellow actor from the Guild days, who put him on to Frank Merlin. Merlin took an option on the play, and on November 27, 1933 it was listed under its new name *(Awake and Sing!)* as a forthcoming production; the author was identified as a member of the cast of *Men in White*. In later press releases, *Awake* was promised for January, but that turned out to be the month of Merlin's fiasco—a disaster, ironically enough, that would not have been possible without a rather ludicrous assist from the Group. Clurman told the story in *The Fervent Years*. While Odets was putting *Blues* on paper in one room of the Group apartment, Lee Strasberg was having them in another. At this time, a Mrs. Eitingon, with $50,000 to invest in the theater and an attraction to the Group, was trying to reach Strasberg, since he was the best known of the directors. Sanford Meisner brought him the news, but somehow—perhaps because he was beset with the odd mixture of indifference, disbelief and despair that touched most of the Group members that winter—Strasberg never got around to calling the lady. The money went to Frank Merlin, "who produced one play with it and bought another." The first was Hugh Stange's *False Dreams Farewell*, which Odets was to remember later as having "something to do with the sinking of the *Titanic* or the *Lusitania*." The ship was actually the fictional S.S. *Atlantia,* trying to set a crossing record although defectively built, and the play, which told the stories of the passengers who drowned, ran for only three weeks after its January 15 opening.

Although Odets's memory may have been a little faulty on details, his *Titanic-Lusitania* recollection is accurate enough, personally and communally, for *Awake* was Merlin's other play and Mrs. Eitingon was the ship that the Group directors, perenially scrounging for money, always hoped was about to come in. It is all so parabolically neat, like an Odetsian anecdote; the playwright who had named Myron's winning horse "Sky Rocket" would, in the face of failed theatrical magic, have had to call the producer "Merlin" and the flopping play *False Dreams Farewell.* Not that Merlin gave up. During the spring of 1934, there were plans afoot for a season of plays at the Little Theatre, of which *Awake* was to be one. The press releases tell the story: *Times,* June 25, the lease on the Little expired; *Times,* August 13, the series of plays "indefinitely" postponed; *Herald Tribune,* December 2, the option on *Awake* dropped. Much later Edith J.R. Isaacs was to remember that "Nobody who knew Mr. Merlin and saw him that summer escaped his praise of the bright new star in the playwriting firmament." He had been unable to find backing for *Awake* because of casting problems (earlier news releases had indicated that no Bessie could be found), Mrs. Isaacs reported, adding wisely, "No company of players picked up casually in the Broadway manner could make those unhappy individuals look and act like a family." *Awake* had, after all, been written for the Group; in the typescript of *Blues* at the Library of Congress, Bessie is sometimes called Stella, presumably because Odets saw Miss Adler in the role long before she played it.

Nathaniel Buchwald, in his review of *Awake* in the *Daily Worker,* trying to find a reason why a play he so disliked should be produced, suggested that it was "the startling success" of *Waiting for Lefty* which induced the Group to put on the earlier play. It is true that *Awake* was not announced for production until January 13, 1935, more than a week after the celebrated *Lefty* opening, and it is believable that *Awake* became more attractive to the Group directors when its author suddenly ceased to be simply a bit-part actor of questionable talent. Harold Clurman did not help matters in *The Fervent Years.* At one point, as if to kill the old charge of bandwagon-climbing, he said, almost casually, that *Awake* "had been in rehearsal about ten days when *Lefty* was first presented;" elsewhere, he capped his story of the intra-Group struggle over *Awake* by saying that its production was announced to the company ("The actors gave forth a shout of joy and threw their costumes in the air") on the closing night of *Gold Eagle Guy,* which, since the Levy play opened on November 28 and ran eight weeks, would have had to be late in January. *Lefty* may have been a consideration, then, and so, too, the Theatre Guild; if Odets's memory serves him, the Guild wanted to do *Awake* as their last production in the 1934-35 season. Most important, the actors simply refused to let the Group close up shop in January as it had in 1933. Despite the opposition of Strasberg ("You don't seem to understand, Cliff. We don't like your play"), the pro-Odets sentiment prevailed. *Awake* would be done and Clurman would direct it.

Awake and Sing! opened at the Belasco Theatre on February 19, 1935. "The notices were legendary," Odets said years later, and so they were. As *Waiting for Lefty* was to become *the* propaganda play of the 1930s, so *Awake and Sing!* was to become the play that most reflected that period's inchoate longing for personal and political triumph. As the play came to represent the decade, the Group at its greatest, Odets at his brave beginning, it was necessary that its initial reception be reinvented, that a legend grow up around those first reviews. It is true that Walter Winchell trumpeted "Bravodets!!!" and reported that the play "kept the first witnesses in their chairs until about 15 curtains had lifted and fallen to the tune of bravos, cheers and applause" (the Group in a publicity throwaway later upped Winchell's fifteen curtain calls to twenty). This was an exception. On the whole, the reviews were favorable but restrained, gravely welcoming a new young playwright into the circle of Broadway seriousness. There was the flood of publicity and gossip described in the first chapter of this book, but it focused on the playwright, not the play. *Awake* had to make its own way, which it did, but it was not the way of commercial success. It played until the summer and reopened briefly in the fall; it went to Philadelphia and, in the spring of 1936, to Baltimore, Chicago, Cleveland, Newark; but its devoted audiences were not the people who created box-office successes. (Alfred Kazin in *Starting Out in the Thirties* recalls "sitting high up in the second balcony of the Belasco".) It was done in New York in Hungarian (1935) and in Yiddish (1938). It was revived by the Group on March 7, 1939 and played in repertory with *Rocket to the Moon*. "The performance of our revival was relaxed to the point of glibness," Clurman said in *The Fervent Years*, but despite the "distinctly inferior" production, the reviewers treated the revival tenderly. It had, after all, survived. And does still.

Most reviewers work by analogy, reaching for the nearest likely comparison. *Spring Song*, by Bella and Samuel Spewack, is so little like *Awake and Sing!* in tone, in texture and, alas, in quality that it might seem surprising—now, reading the two plays side by side—that *Spring Song* turned up in so many of the *Awake* notices. Yet the Spewack play, having opened the October before, was fresh in the reviewers' minds and there are similarities: *Spring Song* is about a Jewish family, a conflict between a strong mother and her children, and its plot hinges on a premarital pregnancy and a forced wedding. Even more unlikely plays were invoked—Rose Franken's *Another Language*, Louis Bromfield's *Times Have Changed*—but all these comparisons served only to say what most of the reviewers said directly—that *Awake and Sing!* is "a family play." It is a *family play* in the best and most complicated sense of that phrase (as I hope to show later), but most of the reviewers meant something much simpler—that the theme was the perennial quarrel between generations and that the devices were familiar ones. Odets admits as much when, in the scene in which Hennie's pregnancy is revealed, he has Myron say, "It's like a play on the stage. . . ." There is never any doubt about the mutual love of Moe and Hennie (we have known about hating lovers since Beatrice savaged Benedick in *Much Ado About Nothing*); the question is only which of the conventional endings we shall have; death (*Spring Song*), separation (*I Got the Blues*), reconciliation (*Awake*). The working out of the plot is obviously of minimal importance to Odets; it is what his characters make of that working-out that counts.

For that reason, he can introduce that familiar family-play chestnut—the will—and, at the level of plot, throw it away completely. He carefully sets up Jacob's suicide. In the quarrel with Bessie in Act I, the old man insists, "But Ralph you don't make like you. Before you do it, I'll die first," and then, the fight over, he retreats to his room, saying, *"with an attempt at humor:* Bessie, some day you'll talk to me so fresh . . . I'll leave the house for good!" A label is hooked to these generalized remarks when, at the beginning of Act II, Scene 1, there is a discussion of depression-induced suicides. In the same scene Jacob entrusts his will to Morty, an occasion to remark that Ralph is the beneficiary, and with so much preparation weighing the old man down he is bound to go off the roof at the end of II, 2. "This is the most progressive movement of events in the play, because it leads to a defined act," John Howard Lawson wrote; "but it has no organic connection with the play as a whole. . . . The grandfather's death does not make Hennie's running away inevitable, nor does it clearly motivate Ralph's new courage and understanding." Lawson is certainly right on the most obvious level, since Ralph gives up the legacy, and perhaps in a more basic way, but—since Ralph thinks Jacob's suicide is forcing him to act ("The night he died, I saw it like a thunderbolt!")—it is the truth or falsity of the play's ending that must decide the centrality of Jacob's death. If the audience can believe that Ralph is awake and singing at the end, the niceties of plot can go hang. A consideration of that ending, however, will have to wait on a look at the situation and the conflict.

"All the characters in *Awake and Sing!* share a fundamental activity," Odets wrote in "The Characters of the Play," the descriptive notes that precede the printed text: "a struggle for life amidst petty conditions." The conditions are clear enough. It is the middle of the Depression; work is scarce, dull, badly paid; simple survival is about as exalted a goal as any of the characters can hope to reach. "Where's advancement down the place?" asks Ralph in the first line of the play. "Work like crazy! Think they see it? You'd drop dead first." The "struggle for life" is more obvious in the retreat from it, the images of escape that blanket the play. Myron is almost a dramatization of Joe's line in *Waiting for Lefty*, "Jeez, I wish I was a kid again and didn't have to think about the next minute." He lives almost completely in the past; his memories may edge forward to Valentino in *The Sheik* (1921), but for the most part he is caught somewhere between San Juan Hill and World War I, constantly invoking Teddy Roosevelt, recalling Nora Bayes at the old Proctor's Twenty-third Street, reaching back to a world in which it was still possible to believe the Horatio-Alger platitudes ("Never mind, son, merit never goes unrewarded"). "There's no more big snows like in the old days. . . . No one hardly remembers any more when we used to have gaslight and all the dishes had little fishes on them." So, he goes, but nostalgic ways are labyrinthine and truth lies around an occasional corner; not that Myron can quite hear his own words when, in describing the Great Blizzard he remembers as a boy, he says, "A silence of death was on the city and little babies got no milk . . . they say a lot of people died that year." When he does emerge from the past, it is not to stop in the present but to move on to a moment when luck will carry him into a comfortable future. To anyone who remembers, as I do, those long Depression evenings when the family gathered around the dining room table, helping father solve that day's installment in the endless newspaper puzzle contest that was going to bring wealth to us all, there is pain as well as humor in Myron's determination to win the Irish Sweepstakes, pick the right horse ("Sky Rocket" indeed), name the "Marvel Cosmetic Girl of Hollywood . . . and win five thousand dollars." In the early part of the play, Ralph is his father's son. With no usable past to escape into, he settles for the might-have-been ("Didn't I want to take up tap dancing, too?") and the undefined lure in the sound of trains in the night, the Boston mail plane passing overhead. And his girl, of course; with less chance of marriage than Sid and Florrie in *Lefty*, he dreams of "Her and me together—that's a new life!" Jacob, looking at himself ("Once I had in *my* heart a dream") and the family around him, warns, "A new death!"

Jacob, of course, has his records. Whenever the infighting gets too intense in the Berger household, he retreats to his room and puts Caruso on the victrola. *"O paradiso* was used by Clifford Odets to symbolize release from frustration in *Awake and Sing,"* Francis Robinson explained in the record notes to *The Best of Caruso.* "It is music to free the spirit." So, it seems to be when Jacob plays the record in Act I and explains it to Moe, " . . . a big explorer comes on a new land—'O Paradiso.' . . . You hear? 'Oh paradise! Oh paradise on earth! Oh blue sky, oh fragrant air—' " But is Odets, the Beethoven lover, doing something a little underhanded—putting a serpent in that paradise—in saddling his character with Meyerbeer and—a little later in the act—Bizet? For Jacob the song has its own context, his longing, as his later use of the lament from *The Pearl Fishers* is a reflection of his own self-pity. Nadir, who sings the lament, may be "the aspiring tenor who is all emotion, no brain and little brawn" as Winton Dean calls him, but for Jacob it is Caruso not Nadir who sings; yet, can the brainless emotionality quite be escaped? When Vasco sings *O paradiso* in *L'Africaine,* the chorus comes in on his happy surprise to call for the death of the strangers; and that paradisiacal island is, first, a prison to Vasco and then the place in which Selika and Nelusko commit suicide. It is such a double-edged symbol that one cannot help supposing—hoping, at least—that Odets intended to let the records themselves undermine their value for Jacob. Such intricacy is too much to expect an audience in the theater to grasp, but Jacob's vulnerability does not hinge on an aesthetic reaction to Bizet or a familiarity with the plot of *L'Africaine.* His records fail him because, like most dreams, they are fragile and Bessie can and does smash them.

What, then, of his Marxist dream? The Odets who wrote the play shared many of Jacob's ideas and, if the ending is successfully positive, those ideas are invigorating Ralph as the curtain comes down. Yet, for Jacob himself, it is just another case of *O paradiso*. Odets describes him in "Characters" as "a sentimental idealist with no power to turn ideal to action," and Jacob describes himself as "A man who had golden opportunities but drank instead a glass tea." The promised revolution, like the Caruso records—both of them jokes in the family—is an imaginary place into which Jacob can escape.

"Your old man still believes in Santy Claus," Moe says to Ralph, after one of Myron's flights, but all roads lead to the North Pole. He calls Hennie "Paradise," insists that she is "home for me, a place to live," wants to carry her off to a cannibal isle (or at least to Havana). "I know a certain place—" he tells Jacob, recalling a summer he once spent lying under orange trees, and the memory, too, is identified with Hennie for at the end of the act, told that she will marry Sam Feinshreiber, he snarls, "What the hell kind of house is this it ain't got an orange!" It is not Moe's tooth-shattering hyperbole (he let the oranges "fall right in my mouth") that makes one suspect that the place never existed outside his mind, but the fact that his orange paradise becomes identified with "the land of Yama Yama" about which he keeps singing, "the place where the good fellows go," and—particularly important to the one-legged veteran who cannot keep his bitterness bottled up—where "You never hear them talk about the war." Anyone in the audience who knows the song, who remembers how the verse begins ("There's a place that you never can trace in Geography"), has an explicit reference, but even the uninitiate can recognize a standard longing-for-escape song when he hears it. Its tone and its date (1917) are just right for Moe. I am a little disturbed—no, intrigued—by the way Odets misquotes—or lets Moe misquote—the chorus. In the actual song, the good fellows *are* there, not still going as they are when Moe sings it. Moe's *Yama Yama* is an inaccurate rendering of *Yamo Yamo*, a not-so-great vowel shift which would be interesting only if "The Yama Yama

Man," a song from Odets's infancy (1908), were sounding in the playwright's or the character's ears. It is a bogeyman song and in a world in which, as Bessie says, "every day furniture's on the sidewalk," the goblins will get you if you don't watch out: "Maybe he's hiding behind the chair, / Ready to spring out at you unaware, / Run to your mama, / For here comes the Yama, Yama man."

Bessie is not completely free of escape images. She is reluctantly drawn to Myron's hope of a long shot ("If they win on Beck Street we could win on Longwood Avenue") and she is a persistent moviegoer. "Someone tells a few jokes," Jacob says, in a line as applicable to the movies as to the vaudeville he is talking about, "and they forget the street is filled with starving beggars." The situation, the family itself, may be a trap for Bessie as much as for the others (as her "I worked too hard" speech in the last act suggests), but she cannot really see it that way. "Talk from now to next year," she says, "this is life in America." For her, the family is the only defense against the economic Yama Yama man who is chewing up households all around her ("They threw out a family on Dawson Street today"), and she is determined to hold them together, to make them a redoubt in a world at war even if she kills them in the process.

Bessie is obviously the strongest character in the play, terrifyingly fierce at times; Rosamond Gilder, reviewing the *Awake* revival, wrote that Julia Adler played Bessie with "a harsh, hysterical emphasis which is undoubtedly right but occasionally wearing." Yet, the character is admirable in her way. In *I Got the Blues* she is much less attractive, simply gross and greedy, but the most imaginative change in the revision of the play is not in what is cut away (her slapping Myron, the revelation that she has money in the bank, her threat to go to her brother Morty) but in what is added—the brief scene with Schlosser in Act I. He is only the superintendent, but to Bessie he is the outsider, the threatening *them,* and she moves between him and her family like a mother tiger shielding her cubs. Before the act is out, her merciless tongue will send Jacob to his room and Caruso's lament, but here she rounds on Schlosser for speaking to him ("Please don't yell on an old man") and praises his intellectual virtues as though they were not the very qualities that ordinarily set her off. Even though the loving destructive Jewish mother has become a painful joke (most noticeably in Philip Roth's *Portnoy's Complaint*), someone reading or seeing *Awake* today would quite likely come away from the play with the feeling that Bessie is the protagonist, but our admiration for her strength, her vitality, her humor should not hide the fact that, in the play, she is defending the indefensible.

"Ah, it's a new generation," sighs Morty, in Act III, and Ralph, who has just entered the room unnoticed, snaps out, "You said it!" There lies the basic conflict of the play. Myron, in some ways the best conceived character in the play, is completely ineffectual. Odets shows this not simply in his memories and his dreams, but in his marvelous sense of irrelevancy ("I see in the papers Sophie Tucker took off twenty-six pounds. Fearful business in Japan"), his disconcerting power to concentrate on the trivial (when Hennie flounces out of the room with "Wake me up when it's apple blossom time in Normandy," he goes into a reverie and comes up, speeches later, with the memory of Nora Bayes singing the song), his irresolution ("Why'd I come in here?" he asks, on entering a room, and immediately exits), even in his sweetness (when Sam, whom nobody likes, says, "Nobody likes me," Myron draws the obvious parallel with, "I like you, Sam"). In *I Got the Blues*, Odets left Myron on stage alone at the end of the play, peeling an apple, the correct visual finish to so negative a play. In *Awake*, he exits early enough to get Ralph's benediction: "Let me die like a dog, if I can't get more from life." Myron, then, is only a sad example. Whether Morty is being sweet (offering Hennie dresses as a way of telling her to shut up) or nasty (interrupting Ralph with, "Keep quiet, snot-nose!"), he is part of the enemy, but he is only a downtown extension of Bessie and the battle is here, in the Berger apartment.

Bessie is the antagonist, the force that Hennie and Ralph must defeat, the magnet away from which they must pull. That much of the play works in the familiar terms of mother-child conflict can be seen in Odets's use of realistic touches which have become conventions in Jewish fiction. At the beginning of the play, when the *kvetching* conversation at table threatens to turn into a real quarrel, Bessie leaps to her feet ("I can't take a bite in my mouth no more"), but she lets Myron reseat her and it is Ralph who runs out of the room, almost in tears. "Myron, your fine Beauty's in trouble," she says, when she discovers Hennie's pregnancy, in a phrase disowning the girl and blaming Myron for being too indulgent; but there are practical matters to see to so she reclaims her daughter with a shift in pronoun ("Our society lady") and still retains the barb — sticks it in Hennie as well—in the rest of the phrase. The best example of all comes in II, 1 when she and Ralph quarrel about his girl. "Miss Nobody should step in the picture and I'll stand by with my mouth shut," she says and when Ralph refuses to give in ("Miss Nobody! Who am I? Al Jolson?"), she argues with perfect mother's logic: "Fix your tie!"

There are, however, more than two generations in this household. Robert Warshow, in his interesting essay on *Awake* as a reflection of the Jewish-American middle class, made the point that the members of the second generation, in response to a marginal family situation, scrambled for money to fulfill an indistinct desire which they could conceive of only in terms of three imperatives: "be secure, be respected, be intelligent." Whether or not this is sound as a generalization, it is certainly a good description of Bessie, and Warshow went on to show how it works dramatically in the play:

> In a brilliant climax, Bessie Berger reveals the whole pattern of psychological and moral conflict that dominates her and her family: when Ralph discovers that his sister's husband was trapped into marriage, Bessie, confronted inescapably with her own immorality, and trembling before her son's contempt, turns upon her *father,* who has said nothing. . . . This act of fury is irrelevant only on the surface: one understands immediately that Bessie has gone to the root of the matter.

Ralph's contempt is clear enough in the scene ("Just have respect? That's the idea?"), but it goes not only to Bessie. It is particularly revealing that her attack on Jacob follows hard on the heels of this exchange:

Myron: I want to tell you—
Ralph: You never in your life had a thing to tell
     me.

Bessie may have been carrying Myron on her back for years, but
the uneasy balance she is trying to maintain makes it necessary
to defend him as well as herself.

There is a somewhat similar situation in Act I when Bessie,
angry and upset over Hennie's pregnancy, attacks Jacob, but
here there is more direct provocation because Jacob has been
protesting her decision to catch Sam as a husband for Hennie. In
this scene, there is a good example of one of Bessie's tactics as a
fighter, a transference technique that has Warshow's "be respected" written all over it. She tries to escape Jacob's accusa-
tion ("The lowest from the low!"), to climb out of the stench of
her decision, to regain respectability, by dismissing him as an
irresponsible critic: "A man who don't believe in God—with
crazy ideas—" When he persists, spits on her idea of respect
("the neighbors' opinion"), she adds that he cannot hold a job.
She does much the same thing in II, 1, when she lies to Ralph
about his phone call and, then, when he insists, becomes outraged: "You call me a liar next." It is not simply a matter of
Bessie's being caught between two generations, both of which
endanger her security; Jacob and the young people are open allies. Jacob declares in Act I that he will fight Bessie to save
Ralph. There is more in his determination than a response to a
difficult daughter. For a Marxist idealist like him (and for the
playwright), Bessie represents something larger than the Jewish
mother.

"The play presents an adjustment in the lives of the characters, not an adjustment of environment," Odets told a New York
Herald Tribune interviewer, sounding as though he, too, thought
it simply a family play, ". . . just a minor family turmoil, an
awakening to life of the characters, a change in attitude." A few
days later, to another interviewer, he insisted on the social
point: "But today the truth followed to its logical conclusion is
inevitably revolutionary. No special pleading is necessary in a
play which says that people should have full and richer lives."
The lines of Morty and Ralph that I quoted, out of context, two

paragraphs back, put the generational conflict in a larger context; Morty's sigh comes after a typical speech of comic disgruntlement at Marx and the troublemakers in Union Square. Morty, the successful businessman, is clearly the stereotypical capitalist not only in his protective speeches (business is bad, the strikers are out to get him) and their juxtaposition with his material well-being ("Where's my fur gloves?"), but in Jacob's reluctant recognition—"aie, Morty" he laments, breaking, at the word "capitalist," the revolutionary rhetoric of the speech he is declaiming at the beginning of II, 2. Bessie, without Morty's advantages, is just as clearly representative of capitalist values:

> Ralph should only be a success like you, Morty. I should only live to see the day when he rides up to the door in a big car with a chauffeur and a radio. I could die happy, believe me.

When Jacob says, "Marx said it—abolish such families," he is not simply expressing his disgust with the dishonesty in Bessie's respectablity. He is echoing the condemnation of the bourgeois family in *The Communist Manifesto:* "The bourgeoisie . . . has reduced the family relation to a mere money relation." The Bergers, as an unhappy unit, are both the victimized result and the tool of the system. "Don't live, just make success," Jacob snorts, shortly after Bessie's speech quoted above. Jacob's pedagogical job in the play is to rescue Ralph from Bessie's conventional wisdom (of all the paradisiacal dreams in *Awake,* success may be the most dangerous), to turn the boy who opens the play worrying about "advancement down the place" into the incipient revolutionary who will not only echo his words, but, hopefully, "Go out and fight so life shouldn't be printed on dollar bills."

There are two revolts against Bessie. Ralph rejects her values, but accepts her challenge: "So go out and change the world if you don't like it." Though he will not "go out;" like Dr. Benjamin in *Lefty,* he will stay and fight on his home ground. Hennie, who is remarkably like Bessie in her tough, wry practicality and her reluctant flirtation with romance, accepts Bessie's values but runs away, hopefully to a better land. The two revolts feed on and affect one another. The final effect of the play depends on how one responds to those revolts and their mutuality. The chief criticisms of the ending of *Awake* have always been that the play itself does not lead inevitably to Hennie's elopement and Ralph's decision, and that their final acts are, in any case, suspicious as optimistic statements. I would like to consider both those problems and, then, go on to what seems to me an even more important consideration—the ending as a theatrical fact.

In his discussion of the play, John Howard Lawson worried about the dramatic development of Hennie, insisting that "we see only her moods" and that there is no real reason why she should run off with Moe in Act III and not in Act I. His argument is somewhat weakened by the fact that he—like a number of other reviewers—assumed, from no evidence within the play, that Moe is the father of Hennie's baby. Otherwise, his is probably the clearest statement of a condemnation that must be considered. Even within the confines of psychological realism, I can make a case for the delay. Moe's invitation is not all that clear at the beginning and Hennie, with the memory of Moe's seducing her and then simply walking away, might be permitted to hesitate; add Sam and the baby to Bessie and the Depression, and the pressure to run is greater in Act III than in Act I. For me, however, this argument is unnecessary. A reviewer like Burns Mantle, who fumed about "synthetic realism" and "a stage family," was on to something about Odets that those who praised the truth of his characters missed. As I suggested earlier in the chapter, Hennie and Moe, whatever surface realism they may carry, are recognizably part of a long line of stage couples; the audience accepts that they love one another from their first fight in Act. I. Theatrical convention will carry them to their final parting or embrace: which it is depends less on manipulation of plot and character than on the tone of the play as a whole. Things necessarily end badly for them in *I Got the Blues*—Moe is arrested just before he convinces Hennie to run away—because defeat smothers that play. The chief argument for their escape in *Awake and Sing!* is the basic genre in which Odets is working ("The mother, of course, has to lose," said Whitney Bolton); the chief argument against it is that Odets transcends the genre, builds an elaborate pattern of failed-paradise images which seems to be pointing toward the frustration of their dream.

There is always the possibility that the fulfilled dream is intended as a failed paradise. Lloyd Morris simply assumed that this is so:

> So, in Odets' plays, youth inevitably rebels. But Odets felt the need of showing that purely personal rebellion—the determination to achieve material satisfaction—is useless; that it is one of the illusions of the dead world of the past, and has no relevance to the new world that must be created.

This is a possibility that can be argued in terms of the destination of Moe and Hennie and what their characters represent beyond two halves of a couple. Presumably, they are going to Havana on one of the cruise ships. The advertisement that Moe tempts Hennie with in II, 1 is tepid compared to the promise of "Havana in *fiesta* mood" that could be found in one of the great number of ads that filled the travel pages of the Sunday New York *Times* (November 25, 1934): "Visit Havana when her year-round play-time season reaches its merriest climax . . ." False paradises are the business of travel advertising, but that fakery is not the point here. At this time Cuba was ruled by the Mendieta-Batista dictatorship (Odets was to make an ill-fated investigatory trip to Havana in the summer of 1935) and, although the tourist business was not seriously hurt, there were sour notes in the *fiesta* music. The president of the Cuban Tourist Commission had to assure travel agents that tourists would be safe in Cuba and, just as Havana was reaching that "merriest climax," the Chief of National Police announced that an English-speaking policeman would accompany each automobile of sightseers, presumably to protect them from beggars, pickpockets and peddlers.

If Havana is a suspicious goal within the social context of the play, so are Hennie and Moe unlikely heroes of optimism. Hennie, as I suggested earlier, shares Bessie's materialistic yearnings, enlarges on them if Moe is correct in his estimate of her ("I know you from the old days. How you like to spend it! . . .

71

Lizard-skin shoes, perfume behind the ears"), and her attitude is cynical from the beginning, not even masked, as Bessie's is, by conventional platitudes. Moe is more ambiguous, compromised by the conflict between what he is and what he does. He is a gangster, but it is not that fact which condemns him so much as the idea for which his racketeering stands. Simple cops-and-robbers movies aside, the gangster was used to represent a variety of things in the 1930s; for instance, he could be a romantic anti-establishment figure (John Wexley's *The Last Mile*) or the last of the rugged individualists (Robert E. Sherwood's *The Petrified Forest*). For Odets, as for Bertolt Brecht in *The Threepenny Opera*, he is a businessman, but it was apparently from John Howard Lawson, rather than Brecht, that Odets got the concept. Sol, the hero of Lawson's *Success Story*, struggling to make it in the business world, sees himself in conscious analogy to his gunman brother ("One-eyed Izzy who got his on Second Avenue"): "This is a gangster's world and I'm out to beat it." Not that Moe needs the Left's gangsterism-capitalism parallel (as far back as Proudhon, property was theft) to define him. He does the job himself in a speech to Morty: "It's all a racket—from horse racing down. Marriage, politics, big business—everybody plays cops and robbers. You, you're a racketeer yourself." As the Moe figure emerges in later Odets plays (Kewpie in *Paradise Lost*, Fuseli in *Golden Boy*), he becomes more specifically this representative figure. Moe is softened, not so much by love for Hennie (after all Kewpie loves Libby, Fuseli loves Joe) as by his rough gentleness with Jacob (their pinochle game in Act I) and his protection of Ralph in Act III. Although I have made Lloyd Morris's case in far greater detail than he did, I do not think Odets really meant the audience to take the Moe-Hennie escape as a bad example—although, if he were rigidly loyal to his social argument, he probably should. He admitted as much in a New York *Times* interview: "I used the conclusion of the two running off to Bermuda [sic] as the solution. But when I wrote it I knew it was a dirty lie." Years later, he was less fierce: "I do believe that, as the daughter in the family does, she can make a break with the groundling lies of her life, and try to find happiness by walking off with a man who is not her husband."

No one, I suspect, can take quite seriously the hint of pro-grammatic action in Ralph's "Coletti to Driscoll to Berger" speech. (Like the strike committee in *Lefty*, this is the American melting-pot in action that we were to see later in all those World War II movies.) It is not what Ralph is going to do, but that he has decided to do something—to act positively, to work for revolutionary change—that the audience must accept if he is to be the "affirmative voice" Odets once called him. As with the Hennie-Moe escape, his decision is called into doubt by the par-adise image-pattern, particularly by the suggestion that, for Ja-cob, the revolutionary dream is only a dream; some critics, such as Mary Virginia Farmer, who found an "unacceptable tone of sweetness and light" in the end, assumed that the Hennie-Moe flight and Ralph's approval of it made his final commitment seem suspiciously immature.

It is not the dangerous analogy of his sister's action or the burden of all those false paradises that most endangers the figure of Ralph as hero. It is the character himself. In one of those sen-tences which even the least imaginative daily reviewer some-times writes, burying an insight in a cluster of factual error, Robert Garland put his finger on the problem: "After all, he leaves his tumultuous young iconoclast occupying the same room, tossing in the same bed and reading the same books that drove the ineffectual old iconoclast who was his progenitor to self-destruction." Ralph does appear, for most of the play, one with his grandfather in weakness rather than in revolutionary thought. This can be seen most clearly at the curtain of II, 1 where they stand in one another's arms, weeping in frustration at their mutual defeat, their humiliation at the hands of Bessie and Morty. Ralph, in the first act, is a whiner, treasuring the wrongs of his childhood: "I never in my life even had a birth-day party. Every time I went and cried in the toilet when my birthday came." Unlike Hennie, whose final acceptance of Moe is implicit in her character from the beginning, Ralph really needs to undergo a change, to get by those second-act tears and on to the third-act resolution.

John Howard Lawson could not accept that change at all, in-sisting, in his critique of the play, that Ralph only tells us "that everything is different." He is right, of course, but Ralph's "telling" is more than the content of his big speeches. It can be heard in his change of tone. There is a wheedling, please-spoil-me quality to his early quarrels with his mother and the pleading can still be heard in his voice in II, 2, when he asks if he can bring Blanche home to live; but that tone disappears a few speeches later, when he discovers his mother's duplicity in Hennie's marriage, and it does not return. This can be seen in two before-and-after examples using repeated references. "It's crazy—all my life I want a pair of black and white shoes and can't get them," he complains at the beginning of the play; in the last act, when it is Bessie who does the pleading, outlining the family's need for the money ("You'll get your teeth fixed—"), he says, ironically, "And a pair of black and white shoes?" In the second act, when he listens to the Boston air mail plane, it is a vague escape symbol, which "cuts across the Bronx"; but in the last act he not only identifies with but redefines it: "Day or night, he flies away, a job to do. That's us and it's no time to die." The difficulty with depending on the sound of Ralph's voice to indicate the change in him is that Odets gives him no positive acts to perform; worse, he keeps him from performing the two that might identify the new him. At the moment of his confrontation with Morty and Bessie in Act III, Moe steps in with the fake suicide note and wins the day for Ralph—but at the boy's expense as a strong figure. A few minutes later, having decided to give up his girl, Ralph takes a call from her, hesitates over it and lets her do the hanging up.

The pages above show quite clearly why even pro-Odets critics have difficulty with the end of the play. The ambiguity which might be applauded in another playwright seems wrong here, I suspect, because the last act is really so effective theatrically. After the curtain is down and the theatergoer is on the subway going home, he may (like the critics) begin to second-guess, convince himself that the Moe-Hennie thing will not last a month, that that sniveling boy will crawl back into his mother's womb—but not while the play is going on. The reason that the ending is so good as a theater piece is that it uses and meshes two quite different romantic devices. Moe and Hennie provide the traditional happy ending for the lovers beset by barriers—real and self-imposed—and her last attempt to resist

him, a no-no-no-maybe-no-no-*yes* sequence, fulfills the expectation of an audience raised on such endings, particularly one
which has just seen a defeated Bessie leave the stage. The other
device is purely rhetorical, the speech to which one responds
not because the way has been laid dramatically, not even because one believes what is being said, but because the spiritual
content—the uplift, to use an unfashionable word—is so com-
manding. I am not ordinarily a susceptible person, but, I confess, that when I reach Ralph's "Right here . . ." speech—even
when reading the play—a shiver of excitement nips at the base
of my spine and I am ready to believe that Ralph will change
the world. A few years ago, I saw at a midwestern university a
production of *Awake and Sing!* which hardly did justice to the
Odets script; yet, when the actor hit "Right here," my shiver
started and, at that moment, the lady sitting beside me, the wife
of the Drama Department head, reached out and clutched my
arm. There may have been a residual attachment to the 1930s in
our reactions, but I assume that the device is effective beyond
such limitations. One of these endings may poison another in
retrospect, as the Farmer review suggested, but, in production,
they should strengthen one another. It is the idealistic Ralph
who pushes the hesitant Hennie into Moe's arms ("I didn't hear
a word, but do it, Hennie, do it!"), and Ralph's speech is set in
the proper practical frame when it gets Moe's benediction: "I
wouldn't trade you for two pitchers and an outfielder."

Given the central conflict of *Awake and Sing!*, it is ironic that
one of its greatest strengths is the depiction of the family. Odets
may not have set out to rescue the Jewish family from the popular theatrical stereotypes that still held the stage, but he did so;
he recognized this when, in the *Herald Tribune* interview, he
said, "There is no radio-type Jewish person in it, and neither are
there any Potash and Perlmutter." In the text of *Potash and
Perlmutter* (1913), the play that Montague Glass and Charles
Klein made from Glass's successful stories about Abe and Maw-
russ, there is little ethnic identification; the verbal jokes are
largely a matter of misused words and misplaced modifiers.
Even the speech in Glass's original stories is, aside from a
sprinkling of Yiddish words, no more than the kind of distortion

one might expect in a newspaper comic like Abe Martin. On stage, presumably, they were played very broadly—standard vaudeville Jews, nineteenth-century caricatures cleansed of implicit anti-Semitism by sentimentality and affection. The efficiency with which the Bergers displaced such characters can be seen from the fact that a revival of *Potash and Perlmutter* in April 1935 (brought on, I suspect, by Odets's mention of it) lasted less than three weeks. Of course, Potash and Perlmutter really belonged to the years before World War I, and Odets only finished a job that time had already begun.

The "radio-type Jewish person" was much more contemporary. Gertrude Berg's show, *The Goldbergs,* began broadcasting in 1929; although it left the air briefly in 1934, so that the cast could do a vaudeville tour, it was obviously *The Goldbergs* to which Odets referred. Anyone who knows the Goldbergs only in their last incarnation on Broadway *(Me and Molly,* 1948), when changing tastes (and presumably, the fact of Odets) had greatly modified Gertrude Berg's early style, cannot understand what Odets was working against. Even at that time, there were those who let the combination of radio and Jewish family confuse them; when the Group players did a scene from *Awake* on the Fleischman Hour, Aaron Stein, who found it one of the "vital moments" on radio, said that "to any devoted radio listener the people of the Odets drama must have recalled radio's own Goldbergs." The reason for that confusion and the unreason in it are immediately apparent if one looks at *The Rise of the Goldbergs* (1931), a collection of Miss Berg's radio scripts, slightly edited to read like stories. "Vat's de matter so late, Sammy?" Mollie asks. "Playing marbles, ha? For vat is your fadder slaving for vat I'm esking you? A marble shooter you'll gonna be? A beautiful business for a Jewish boy?" Neither the sentiments ("You mean we shouldn't have food in the house, but you'll make a jig on the street corner?") nor the strategies (the inducement of guilt) are that far from Bessie Berger's, but it is impossible to imagine Bessie with a mouthful of *vats* and *esks* or with one of Mollie's incredible malapropisms: "Maybe he got himself runned over by a cabsitac. Dey run around so fast like cackroachers." This is verbal humor at the expense of a real language, and it is used, perhaps unintentionally, to destroy any suggestion of validity in the characters and the situation. Odets manages to find the humor in the language and retain the psychological truth of the family. That is why Robert Warshow could call him the "Poet of the Jewish Middle Class" and Alfred Kazin could remember "Sitting in the Belasco, watching my mother and father and uncles and aunts occupying the stage . . . by as much right as if they were Hamlet and Lear."

Awake and Sing!, however, creates a family in a more complicated sense than the believable presentation of a milieu. At this point, it is Chekhov, not Gertrude Berg, that has to be held up for comparison; and therein lies a problem. Ever since *Awake* first opened, Chekhov has been brought in to shore up Odets or to beat him down. "A bit of loose talk about Chekhov's influence on Odets cropped up in some reviews," Harold Clurman wrote, primly, in *The Fervent Years*, quite ignoring that it was the Group which started the whole thing; a pre-opening interview with Morris Carnovsky reported that some members of the Group thought Odets "the nearest thing to Tchekov" and others called him the "Sean O'Casey of America." Clurman belonged in the second faction as his introduction to the published play indicated. Since the reviewers first bit at this Group bait, it has been customary in Odets criticism to say *Chekhov* as though the name were a grigri and something was explained by mentioning it. Still, a comparison will help, so long as there is no attempt to equate the dramatic method of the two playwrights (Chekhov retains his enclosure; Odets tries to break out and up) and no need to measure one against the other. Oddly enough it was Stark Young, usually fastidious and fragile in the face of Odets, who stated that comparison most neatly: "Mr. Odets' likeness to Chekhov lies, first, in his use of the method of the seemingly irrelevant. Speech and emotion follow one on another without any surface connection." The connections, in Chekhov and in Odets, were made long before the play began. The Bergers (like the Prosorovs) know one another so well that they hear a line before it is spoken, answer it by rote if at all, never hear the disparity between one line and the next. Even their explosions are familiar so that two characters can clash and, then, subside without breaking the normal rhythm of the conversation about them. This is a family in the truest, the most comfortable (perhaps the most stultifying) sense, and it is this creation that is the major triumph of *Awake and Sing!*

Mary Virginia Farmer, commenting on this quality in her *New Theatre* review ("the relations and connections of scene and feeling and character are often hidden and subtle, arrived at unexpectedly"), wondered at the demands such a play made on the performers and was pleased to see how well they were fulfilled. It is possible that the demands were the other way around. The company came before the play and, as I pointed out in Chapter II, the Group was a family of sorts for Odets and one for which he consciously wrote. The family, then, becomes a playing area, familiar, limited, peopled with knowable qualities. Although none of the plays that followed have quite the texture that *Awake and Sing!* manages, all of them (particularly those he wrote during the 1930s with the Group players in mind) have an "at home" quality about them which is the more remarkable considering that Odets's theme is often homelessness, displacement. Odets's characters are, first of all, on stage, in an environmental context; only then are they involved in an action. In creating the Berger family, Odets found a playwriting technique.

A word on the characters. It is customary to praise Odets for his fidelity to nature, but it is even more important to recognize that he works from type. Truth, on stage, is frequently a matter of giving verisimilitude to stock characters. There are two obvious reasons why this should be true. First of all, we tend to see people (in reality as well as on stage) as types. Second, a stock character is as much an actor's as a playwright's tool; it is a point of departure which can lead an actor to cartoon or to humanity. I can imagine a production of *Awake* that would reduce Bessie Berger to a Syd Hoff cartoon and another that would turn her into an intricately suffering human being. Neither would be completely false to Odets, since Bessie is both type and individual, but the first would dehumanize the script and the second would quite likely obscure the ideational, the thematic play. Odets never worked as a strict realist; what his characters say and do has a meaning beyond the word, the act. For that reason, types have always been useful to him. This is obvious in the way the characters in *Awake and Sing!* recur in later plays: the ineffectual old man, the gangster, the wry ki-bitzer (another side of Moe), the Jewish mother, the inoperative idealist, the young man stepping into life.

If Odets's characters come from the stage as well as from life, so, too, his language. He may have had a perfect ear for collo-quial speech, as many reviewers suggested, and he may have "sat in bars taking notes, and, for *The Flowering Peach*, resorted to the tape recorder itself," as Eric Bentley reported in *The Life of the Drama;* but his dialogue is artificial in the best sense of that word—a literary creation using and transcending idiomatic speech and conveying a vivid sense of actuality. When the audi-ence poured out of the theater after the first performance of *Waiting for Lefty*, delighted at having heard their own voices on stage, they were probably responding as much to the absence of formal literary language and flat undecorated stage speech as to the vernacular truth of what they had heard. When Robert Lewis told me the story of that fabled night, the line he gave as an example was Sid's description of his brother as "that dumb basketball player," a phrase that Stanley Burnshaw picked out in his *New Masses* review as an instance of overdoing the idiom. For Burnshaw, that line "all but undermines the poignancy of the scene," but the response of Lewis's remembered audience is probably more trustworthy (the phrase at once reflects and masks Sid's feeling for his brother and is certainly more charac-teristic). It is the slightly oblique, mockingly overstated quality of Odets's language that has been most celebrated.

Although American farce has always used a style very like Odets's—the wisecrack hiding the heart—the immediate source of his language is clearly John Howard Lawson. Odets has said that *Success Story* had "a very decisive influence on me, by showing me the poetry that was inherent in the chaff of the street." What that statement, as condescending as it is pompous, means is that Lawson taught him that a serious play could use lines like, "You can't fire me, I've quit" and "That's Christian of you, but you see I'm Jewish and miserable." It was a lesson Odets learned well. The language in *Success Story* in nonde-script compared to the color, the humor, the variety in *Awake and Sing!*

It is easier to recognize an Odets line than to characterize one. Commentators have a way of going soft-headed when they try to describe Odets's speech; even so intelligent a critic as Clurman takes refuge in adjectives ("tenderly defiant") or nouns ("vulgarity, tenderness, energy, humor and a headlong idealism are commingled") that caress rather than clarify. It might be simpler to list some of the ingredients of Odets's speech and the verbal devices he uses in *Awake and Sing!*; a sample is not a definition, but it is a step on the way. Although there is practically no Yiddish (Morty's "shtupped," Bessie's "Noo?") in the play, the locutions ("You gave the dog eat?") reflect the Berger family background. There is a great deal of quite ordinary slang ("it rained cats and dogs"), some of it very old-fashioned ("The cat's whiskers"). Although Odets is capable of making a mess of his slang (Joe in *Lefty* has nothing to eat all day but "A coffee and java"), he usually uses it well, laying a foundation on which he can build. Sam's use of "second fiddle" becomes Bessie's "By me he don't even play in the orchestra"; the baseball slang progresses from the expected ("All I want's a chance to get to first base!" "Don't be a bush leaguer") to the hyperbolic ("I wouldn't trade you for two pitchers and an outfielder"). Familiar expressions ("So go fight City Hall") abound, some of them environmental adaptations (Bessie's "Another county heard from" was "Another province heard from" when Golde used it in Sholom Aleichem's *Tevye's Daughters*), others altered for the occasion ("What this country needs is a good five-cent earthquake"). There are references to movies ("What do I do—go to night-clubs with Greta Garbo"), the funnies ("a real Boob McNutt"), popular songs. My favorite example of the latter is Edna's "A cottage by the waterfall, roses in Picardy" in *Lefty*, in which two songs—a World War I favorite and a popular new number from *Footlight Parade* (1933)—are telescoped to form a single dead-dream line.

Such a cultural mix is less startling today than it was in the 1930s, but even then the happy surprise was less in the material that went into the Odets line than in his manipulation of it. He uses a great deal of figurative language and with great variety. Bessie's lines can be as practical as she is ("He should try to buy a two-cent pickle in the Burland Market without money") or almost surreal ("He opens his mouth and the whole Bronx could fall in"). A metaphor, like Moe's "Now you got wings, kid," can work idiomatically for the character yet extend itself suggestively as the audience recognizes that Jacob's legacy to Ralph is not simply money. A conventional simile can be pulled awry by a neighboring verb: "They got you pasted on the wall like a picture, Jake." That line is Moe's and he is the character with whom Odets is most inventive, giving him blunt, direct lines whose impact depends on odd shifts in context (moving a discussion of *change* from the abstract to the practical: "The only thing'll change is my underwear") or inexplicable connections ("You ain't sunburnt—you heard me"). A good many of the lines get their vitality not simply from the verbal surprises they contain, but from the dramatic context, the distance between what they say and what they *really* say. Florrie's "French and Indian War" line in *Lefty* is an example of a favorite device of Odets's, the answer that tries to demolish the question with absurdity—not because the character resents the question so much as he fears the truth that he would have to face in a direct answer. *Awake* is full of such exchanges, particularly in the scene in which Hennie's pregnancy is discovered. To Bessie's "Tell me what happened," Hennie: "Brooklyn Bridge fell down." To Bessie's "Who's the man?" Hennie: "The Prince of Wales." To Bessie's "Where are you going?" Hennie: "For my beauty nap, Mussolini. Wake me up when it's apple blossom time in Normandy." It is Hennie who gets to deliver most of the sharp answers, not only in this scene but throughout the play. One of the best comes at the beginning of Act III where she answers Sam's "Why should you act this way?" with "Cause there's no bones in ice cream," a line in which she admits the extent of her defeat even while she is saying *buzz off*. All of Hennie's answers are examples of the way in which Odets lets his characters mask their feelings, but no question-and-answer sequence is needed to call the smoke-screen lines into play. The most famous example is Moe's complaint about the orangeless house at the end of Act I; the most explicit is his "Listen, lousy," in II, 1, which the stage direction says should be delivered *"as if saying 'I love you.' "* If the characters choose not to hide their feelings, as likely as not they go lyrical, sometimes distressingly so: "Boy, I'm telling you I could sing! Jake, she's like stars.

She's so beautiful you look at her and cry! She's like French words!" This is Ralph, in love for the first time, but even Moe can go that road, as when he compares Hennie to "Ted Lewis playing the clarinet—some of those high crazy notes!"

Odets's dialogue pattern was set in *Awake and Sing!* In later plays, there were modifications, occasional attempts to build a whole character on verbal style (Hoff in *The Big Knife*), but the devices remained and, so too, the almost suicidal grandiosity. There are Odets lines so outrageous that they pull one up short (as the "dumb basketball player" line did Burnshaw), almost stopping the scene. Odets is painfully easy to parody (see "Waiting for Santy," in S. J. Perelman's *Crazy Like a Fox*), but there is little point in it. An Odets line, when it misses, is itself parody so fine that it would make a professional parodist's mouth water. Otis Ferguson said as much years ago when, in his review of *Six Plays*, he shuddered over a *Lefty* line, Sid's "Christ, Baby! I get like thunder in my chest when we're together." My own favorites are two of what I think of as Odets's fruit-salad lines: Carrie's "You might take a lesson from the lowly banana, Mrs. Finch—stick to your bunch or you'll get skinned!" *(The Silent Partner)* and Rita's "What am I? A bowl of fruit? A tangerine that peels in a minute?" *(Sweet Smell of Success)*. As soon as I had written the lines above, I realized that I was not quoting simply to make a critical point, but out of real affection. Even Odets's bad lines are likable. His good ones, his best ones provide the pleasure of audacity and, then, as the implications begin to register, feed back into the play, enriching character, situation, theme.

V. *"with brutal sentimentality"*

WHEN, AFTER the opening of *Awake and Sing!*, the Group Theatre decided to move *Waiting for Lefty* to Broadway, it apparently occurred to no one to honor those other playwriting Group actors, Elia Kazan and Art Smith, by bringing *Dimitroff* along. A conscious decision to ignore the earlier agitprop would have been sound on aesthetic and practical grounds, but Harold Clurman—who did an influence reversal bit in *The Fervent Years* when he said that Art Smith's post-*Lefty* labor play, *The Tide Rises*, "showed the Odets influence already at work"—gave no indication that he knew *Dimitroff* existed. When Odets sat down to turn out a companion piece for *Lefty*, he may have acknowledged the work of his two friends by choosing to write an anti-Nazi play. Of course, it was a logical subject to choose. During 1934, as a glance through the pages of *New Masses* and *New Theatre* would indicate, the Left had shown a growing preoccupation with Nazi Germany. Not the Left alone. The first anti-Nazi plays, disasters all, reached Broadway in the season of 1933–34—Adolph Phillipp's adaptation of Theodore Weachter's *Kultur*, Richard Maibaum's *Birthright* and Leslie Reade's *The Shatter'd Lamp*. In the fall of 1934, more serious, more highly respected playwrights turned to the subject—Elmer Rice with *Judgment Day* and S. N. Behrman with *Rain From Heaven*. Since Rice had disguised his Nazis as mythical Balkans and

Behrman had chosen to work in his usual drawing-room setting, the time was ripe for a direct propaganda assault. Who better to make it than the most celebrated young radical playwright in America and what better occasion.

Till the Day I Die was "a hasty job—done in four nights," Odets told Percival Wilde in a letter quoted in Wilde's introduction to the play in *Contemporary One-Act Plays from Nine Countries* (1936). This hurry is still obvious in the printed and reprinted *(Six Plays)* script, not simply in the play's artistic deficiencies, but in the kind of sloppiness that lets the stage directions for Scene IV read "The same as 3," when the set of II is called for, and that fails to sort out the confusions that arise when one compares the cast list to the actual characters. (The discrepancy in the second case and an apparent reference in Scene V to the Soviet-French pact of May 2 suggest that the printed text may not be the one first performed.) *Day*, directed by Cheryl Crawford, and *Lefty* opened at the Longacre on March 26, 1935. With a few exceptions—Richard Watts, Jr. in the New York *Herald Tribune* and Edith J. R. Isaacs, who called it "so far ahead of anything else that Odets has done . . . that it escapes comparison with them"—the reviewers dismissed *Day* by attacking it, ignoring it or offering yes-but praise to the playwright for tackling the subject. The play ran for 136 performances, well into July, but it was presumably the *Lefty* half of the bill that sustained the run.

Although *Day* never had the vigorous post-Broadway life that *Lefty* did, it became a usable anti-Nazi play for workers' theaters, and it had its small share of trouble from censors, official and unofficial. In Philadelphia, for instance, the New Theatre was kept from staging it in April 1935 by the threat of having its license revoked. The most dramatic incident occurred in Los Angeles where William Ghere (now Will Geer), who was directing the *Lefty-Day* double bill in a small theater, was kidnapped by four "Friends of New Germany" and severely beaten; according to *Variety*, his "Attackers told Ghere they objected to a scene where Hitler's picture is torn from the wall." Merit aside, one possible reason why *Day* was never as popular as *Lefty* is the confusion that must have affected potential producers in the face of the Leftist attempt to be at once pacifist and anti-Nazi.

The conflict—so obvious in retrospect in names like League Against War and Fascism and "Anti-Fascist and Peace" (a category in the New Theater League's 1938 catalogue of plays)—must have worked, however unconsciously, on the theater group which had to choose between disowning war with Albert Maltz (*Private Hicks*) and Irwin Shaw (*Bury the Dead*) and joining Clifford Odets in an implicit call to arms.

In the making of *Till the Day I Die*, as in the writing of *Waiting for Lefty*, Odets used whatever material came to hand. He admitted, in his letter to Percival Wilde, that "the genesis of many of the ideas used is hazy in my mind." That explains the complications about the "letter" in *New Masses* on which the play was admittedly based ("To be blunt, it sounds like it," snarled Richard Lockridge). After acknowledging the "letter" in the program and in a note accompanying the published play, Odets discovered—when he was approached for royalties—that what he remembered as a letter had been a short story in letter form. During 1934, *New Masses* occasionally ran a column "Voices from Germany," in which anecdotes, often fictional, were printed. On more than one occasion excerpts from F. C. Weiskopf's *Those Who are Stronger* appeared (the book, *Die Stärkeren* was published in Prague that year), and it was one of these that gave Odets the starting point for *Day*. What he got from Weiskopf were the details of the way the Nazis worked to break down the captured underground worker (the pattern of torture and release) and to make him appear a traitor to his friends (forcing him to accompany the Radical Squad on raids, stationing him at the door so that prisoners on the way to cross-examination would see him, providing him with new clothes to make him look like a paid stool-pigeon, issuing a bogus underground leaflet accusing him of selling out). The protagonist of the Weiskopf story breaks and informs and, presumably with his own blessing, is killed by his brother. In *Day*, Ernst Tausig commits suicide to keep from breaking; thus Odets converts Weiskopf's theme of revolutionary discipline to one of self-discipline.

Odets's debt to Weiskopf is a great deal less than that to Karl Billinger (Paul W. Massing). Billinger's name turned up first in

Richard Watts's column, which found the recently published *Fatherland* similar in tone to Odets's play. Early the next year, in his attack on *Paradise Lost,* James T. Farrell said bluntly that *Day* "was based on notes from Billinger's *Fatherland.*" To Percival Wilde, who listed many of the borrowings in his introduction, Odets admitted that he may have seen a chapter of the Billinger book in *New Masses.* Indeed, he had. Since the book came out in March 1935, it would have been possible for Odets to have seen an advance copy of it, but all the evidence points to "In the Nazis' Torture House" (*New Masses,* January 1, 1935) as the source for most of Scene III of *Day.* This is an abridged and heavily edited version of Chapter II ("Columbia") of *Fatherland,* but everything that Odets used is in the *New Masses* version. Some of the borrowing is very direct. The stage directions for the scene (the card-playing, beer-drinking guards, the prisoners lined along the wall, the guns and blackjacks on the table) come from Billinger, as do two of the sequences—the young trooper's knocking down the old man, the tormenting of the boy caught delivering pamphlets. Even the lines—particularly in the second case—come directly from Billinger. The contest between the first and second troopers, to see which can knock his man down first, is a dramatization of a practice that is only described in *Fatherland,* and other incidents (the abusing of the World War I veteran, the typing mix-up from Scene II) appear to be based on comments elsewhere in the chapter. Wilde suggested that the "nucleus of the first scene" came from Billinger's few lines on mimeographing, but such an assumption—which depends on Odets's having read more than the *New Masses* excerpt—is unnecessary since Weiskopf's Martin also ran an underground press.

Despite the extensive pilfering from Billinger, *Till the Day I Die* is plainly Odets's play—not so much because there are occasional exchanges that are unmistakenly his (Tilly: "He's your brother." Carl: "That won't sell a postage stamp!"), as because the propaganda impulse of the play is tempered by a theatricality that sentimentalizes heroes and villains alike.

Essentially, *Day* is the story of Ernst Tausig, although it is told less in terms of what he does (until he pulls the final trigger) than in what is done to him. Scene I establishes, in a few lines, his love for Tilly, his affection for his brother Carl, his easy friendship with the other workers. That done, the arrest takes place and we are ready for his testing. Although his violin-playing hand is smashed in Scene II and he is beaten in Scene III, he really has no existence as a character in Scenes II through IV, for these are exhibition scenes (see the Nazi horrors!) in which Ernst is either ingredient or observer. Although Scene V has some of the excitement of a thriller in its last few minutes, as Tilly and Carl outsmart the police, and a presumably touching meeting between Ernst and Tilly, it is largely expositional, continuing the account, begun by Major Duhring in Scene IV, of how Ernst will be used. Ernst is of course not in Scene VI, the meeting at which, on Carl's plea and with Tilly's reluctant vote, he is blacklisted. He returns in the final scene, a broken man—despised by Carl, who thinks he has informed, and pitied by Tilly—with just strength enough to clear his name (for the sake of the baby Tilly is carrying) and to protect the cause by committing suicide. "Let him die," Carl says at the end and, after the shot, "Let him live."

At one level, Ernst's story is a Communist cautionary tale like Bertolt Brecht's *Die Massnahme* (1930), an exercise in revolutionary theory in which the individual must be willing to sacrifice himself for the group: "*You* did not pronounce the verdict: / Reality did." This is presumably the point of Carl's speech in VI, his insistence that "There is no brother, no family, no deeper mother than the working class." Yet *Till the Day I Die* is not a *Lehrstück,* as *Die Massnahme* is, not a didactic play designed more for the performers than the audience. For all its Communist orientation, *Day* is a propaganda play that wants to use Ernst's story to convince an audience of outsiders of the evils of Nazism and of the need of a united front to fight Germany. As such, it embodies two contradictions—one structural, one ideational. The play about party loyalty implicit in Ernst's suicide is not the best vehicle for a direct anti-Nazi statement; after all, one of the forces driving him to death is the "spy-psychosis," as Billinger called it, the climate of suspicion that marks the underground organization. Within the propaganda play, it is difficult to decide whether we are to be moved toward Ernst's dreams of a future when "Brothers will live in the soviets of the world," or toward the action implicit in Major Duhring's " 'Red Front' I can't say to you. . . . But 'United Front'—I say that." Are the *for* (the Communist future) and the *against* (the Nazis) of the play inseparable? It is as though the play were teetering between the old Communist line of exclusiveness ("If you want to register an emotional protest against Nazi polity, Mr. Odets requires that you join the Communist brethren," wrote Brooks Atkinson) and the Popular Front, which would not become official until it was blessed the next August by the Seventh World Congress of the Communist International. Perhaps Odets had not gone beyond lip service to cooperation, as Bill Shulman insisted in *Socialist Call:* "It remained for Odets to present to the American audience the only united front an American Communist can conceive, a united front of members of only the Communist Party." In any case, the neat line—politically and dramatically—of *Waiting for Lefty* is missing in *Day* which may be why Odets had to end it with Carl's sentimental rhetoric rather than an equivalent of the STRIKE! cry.

For the most part, *Day* was taken simply as an *against* play, an anti-Nazi statement. There are problems with that reading in both the positive characters and the Nazis themselves. Since Ernst and his friends oppose the Hitler regime from the beginning, there is no conversion with which the audience can identify, by which it can be drawn into the fight. In fact, the plot, insofar as it works at all, leads the audience into defeat and destruction. Ernst's suicide is supposed to be a positive act (like the one in *The Big Knife*), but, robbed of its Brechtian message, it is simply a romantic gesture and understood as such only because audiences have a latent attachment to what might be called the Sydney Carton syndrome. Certainly, Ernst has little existence as a character. He cannot survive on idiosyncrasies (like the man with one shoe off at the meeting, or the tulip-loving Baum) and he is never realized in depth. One reason is that Ernst's scenes are not self-contained (like those in *Lefty*, like the Nazi scenes here) but depend on an emotional freight that he needs to bring into them but that he never has. Another is that he and Tilly and Carl sound like posters when they speak about the future or the cause. Compare the last line of *Fatherland*, the wry "Come on, back to the trenches!" (which might have come out of *Awake and Sing!*) with Carl's benediction over Ernst. At most, Ernst comes through as a demonstration piece. We see him in three stages: whole, breaking, broken. If he is to serve the propaganda play at all, it is as victim not exemplar.

What of the Nazis who destroy him? Although they do terrible things in the play, they come across as not very formidable. The casual violence of the troopers in Scene III is the most frightening since it reflects the too familiar behavior of minor power figures in an environment which condones official violence. It is framed, however, by two comic exchanges between Peltz and Weiner, Odets's addition to his Billinger borrowing, which rob the central section of force by insisting—look, stage comics, stage violence. Funny Nazis abound. Popper, the detective, is a comic turn, a frustrated authoritarian figure whom no one accepts as such. If the leaflet-reading at the beginning of Scene IV were not evidence enough that Edsel and Martin are a misplaced vaudeville team, the assumption would be confirmed by the fact that Robert Lewis (as Martin) made himself up to look like one of the Three Little Pigs. Perhaps the other Nazi characters (Duhring aside) were also to be played for laughs. Frau Duhring is obviously a broad caricature and her first slapping Ernst and then fastidiously discarding her glove is ludicrous ("the author wishes to make her contemptible," Wilde said, "yet he succeeds only in making her impossible"). Leon Alexander in his *Daily Worker* review said that the humor, which he found "tedious and nasty," was "directed mainly at homosexuality," which would make even Captain Schlegel comic. There would be a precedent; the first scene of *Dimitroff*—in which Goebbels fondles van der Lubbe while he, Goering and Hitler instruct the boy about burning the Reichstag—is presumably a joke.

Yet the play was obviously not funny, nor intended to be. It is simply that the ineffectuality implicit in the comic figures lessens the Nazis as opponents; and the caricaturing technique, used in conjunction with those comic figures, infects all the others, turning them into grotesques as well. Schlegel's homosexuality (which would have been an expected touch any time after the Ernst Roehm purge) allows for a kind of mock delicacy which heightens the falseness of his sadistic bit in Scene II (crushing Ernst's hand while talking about Beethoven's Opus 61). His verbal duel with Duhring casts doubt on that character—if the idea of a Communist, Jewish Nazi, lured into the service of Hitler because of his marriage, is not already a bit thick. Perhaps I am looking back on the play from the vantage point of all those wartime movies when variations on Schlegel (the cultured sadist) and Duhring (the anti-Nazi Nazi) crowded the screen, but I think not. Even at the time reviewers recognized that Odets was exposing the Nazis, as Percy Hammond put it, "with brutal sentimentality." The play does not fail because the characters are unrealistic, but because the artificiality does not work in a total artistic context, as it does in *Awake and Sing!*; instead, as the play moves from comedy to brutality to sentiment, the theatricality imposes the kind of overstatement that makes one doubt not only the immediate dramatic experience but the objective situation that it is trying to uncover. As a practical propaganda play, *Day* is deficient because it gives a valid artistic reason for any ostrich in the audience to hide his head. On the other hand, those willing to recognize the dangers of Nazism are falsely comforted by the play's excessive reliance on sentimental melodrama. Major Duhring's suicide scene, like the killing of the Hitler figure at the end of Rice's *Judgment Day*, is a theatrical solution to a non-theatrical problem. "This is all wish-fulfillment," wrote Rudolf Wittenberg in one of the most perceptive commentaries written on the play.

Unlike *Waiting for Lefty*, in which the specific situation can be generalized, *Till the Day I Die* is inescapably fixed in 1935. Probably the weakest of Odets's plays, it is interesting largely because—a few sketches aside—it is his last piece of pure propaganda and—since *The Silent Partner* and *The Cuban Play* were not produced—his last public attempt to deal directly with an important social situation. It exposed not only the Nazis, but his own limitations.

VI. *"I guess failure's gone to my head"*

P ARADISE LOST, poorly received as a practical theatre work, remains my favorite play in this group," Clifford Odets wrote in the Preface to *Six Plays*. Years later, he was to reaffirm his affection: "It's too jammed, too crowded, it spills out of its frame, but it is in many ways a beautiful play, velvety; the colors were very gloomy and rich."

Burns Mantle may have exaggerated when he reported that Odets "looked at his first check and went to his room to start work on 'Paradise Lost,'" but the play was begun in 1933 at about the time Frank Merlin took his option on *Awake and Sing!* By the end of the year, the first two acts were finished. At least in its first form then, *Lost*, like *Awake*, predates the propaganda plays, a fact that may explain the apparent conflict between the play and its ending. That ending was presumably not written until long after the play was begun, for Harold Clurman said in *The Fervent Years* that Odets, in the busyness of his first success, did not get around to revising the third act until the play had been in rehearsal for three weeks. Under Clurman's direction, *Lost* opened at the Longacre Theatre on December 9, 1935 and was greeted by a devasting critical attack—or so it seemed to Odets and the Group. In retrospect, the notices as a whole do not seem that damning; the reviewers found the play confusing and overambitious, certainly not what they hoped for from Odets, but they did not write him off for that reason. He was still the young hopeful. There was a high degree of acidity scattered through the reviews, but that may have arisen from a tactical error on the part of Helen Deutsch, the publicity representative of the Group. According to Clurman, it was her idea that Odets write an article (a version of it was printed, post-opening, in the New York *Times*) elucidating, as the *Times* title had it, "Some Problems of the Modern Dramatist." He explained that his interest in *Awake* had been "not in the presentation of an individual's problems, but in those of a whole class," and that now, in *Lost,* "The hero . . . is the entire American middle class of liberal tendency." He compared himself to Chekhov, dismissed the conventions of the post-Ibsen theater, and discarded plot completely: "Excuse us for not showing the gun in the first act, because it will later be used in the second." The article was sent around to the reviewers before the play opened and even those who did not resent being lectured to by the playwright could go to their typewriters primed for an argument. It was probably Odets's comments on the middle class as much as the play itself that dictated the shape of the most brutal review the play received—Joseph Wood Krutch's "The Apocalypse of St. Clifford" in the *Nation.*

The Group flew to the play's defense. Clurman prepared, as he said in *The Fervent Years,* "a kind of protest and rebuke of the press which was widely published and, in several instances, answered." Clurman's main point was that *Lost,* being ambitious, deserved a different, a more understanding press coverage than that given the usual Broadway farce. It was Krutch's answer that was most pointed: "to prefer a pretentious play which doesn't come off to an unpretentious one which does is not to demonstrate a refinement of feeling and an exalted mind; it is merely to reveal oneself as a highbrow, a prig, and a 'serious thinker.'" Still chafing months later, in an interview, datelined Hollywood, Odets dismissed all critics (except Clurman) and said specifically of Krutch: "No wonder he lost his temper. While he was sitting there watching it, the whole play kept saying to him, 'You're dead, Krutch; you're dead.'" Clurman was still fighting the fight in *The Fervent Years,* assuming of *Lost* that "not its gloom but its hope" offended Krutch, the pessimist "who had written the woeful *Modern Temper.*" The quarrel between Krutch and Clurman-Odets was not a peripheral one; it was central to the controversy that *Paradise Lost* evoked. One might have expected Stanley Burnshaw to respond to Krutch's "so Mr. Odets has lost his reason . . . from too much brooding on the Marxian eschatology," by insisting, "It is the lack of Marxism which has deprived the play of its fundamental social truth," but it was not the weeklies alone that cited Krutch. Both Brooks Atkinson and John Mason Brown pointed to the *Nation* review in columns in which they defended their initial reactions. The play's friends did not help. Heywood Broun, in finding Odets "a far greater figure than O'Neill," provided another point for quibbling. (Clifton Fadiman's assertion that Odets took the problem play beyond the "narrow range of Ibsen" came too late to join the fray.) In all of this, there were several fights going on at once: a political (or was it spiritual) quarrel over social optimism; the standard assumption that the critics approached casually what was both art and life to theater professionals; the basic problem of how many points good intentions should count in a critic's perfectability scale; the simple difference of opinion about whether it was a good or bad play.

The sad thing was the economic context in which the discussion took place. American plays are always forced to defend their artistic virtue while trying to stay alive. Odets's reactions reflect this ambiguous struggle. In Robert Garland's column, Odets pointed to Lewis Corey's *The Crisis of the Middle Class,* which he said "backs up with cold statistics and philosophical abstracts the human content" of *Lost,* and at the same time retreated from his original Chekhov analogy, a naughty boy sheepishly admitting that he had been bragging: "You have my word for it that I intend to read 'The Cherry Orchard' tonight for the first time in my life." To Richard Watts Jr., who generally admired the play, Odets wrote an intelligent refutation of several of his criticisms, but marred the soundness of his remarks with a conventional anti-critic dig, his assumption that it was not the play but the speed with which it followed *Awake* on Broadway that governed their reviews. Odets complained in a letter to Theodore Dreiser about how the playwright is forced to be a salesman; yet, his exchange with Dreiser (in the Dreiser Collection

93

at the University of Pennsylvania) is an amusing example of the artist-salesman in action. In response to a telegram from Odets, Dreiser went to see *Lost* and, under the assumption that criticism was what Odets wanted, wrote a long letter praising the play, yet outlining its faults. Odets, who really only wanted a usable quote, could not keep from arguing the points in his answer to Dreiser, although he did get around to asking if he might use a version he had prepared of Dreiser's praise of the play. Dreiser gave permission, but, after all Odets's work, the quotation was apparently not used.

A similar mixed motive can be seen in the advertisements that the Group took out to counteract the first reviews. An elaborately bordered announcement appeared in the *Times,* the *Herald Tribune* and the *World-Telegram* for December 11, in which what I accept as a genuine statement of faith ("We believe Clifford Odets' 'Paradise Lost' is a great and important play. We are proud to present it") is shored up with conventional fake quotations culled from negative reviews (from Atkinson and Percy Hammond); a variation in the *News* for December 13 added still more unlikely reviewers' plugs. Even such intellectual activities as a forum at the 92nd Street YMHA on " 'Paradise Lost' and the Modern Drama" with Clurman, John Gassner and Alexander Kirkland, and Clurman's interesting *New Theatre* article on the play and its directorial problems were publicity of a sort. Despite the controversy, the original negative reviews prevailed. Even with salary cuts and lowered ticket prices, the Group could keep the play going for only seventy-three performances. It closed during February, the month in which Odets finally gave in to the blandishments of Hollywood.

"If it were less realistically described, one might suspect the author of symbolism. As realism it is ridiculous, comic exaggeration," wrote Richard Lockridge. "Odets' play is so obviously symbolistic and not realistic, that I marvel at the rather pedestrian approach some of the critics have taken," said Michael Gold. John Gassner, getting the best of both worlds (and incidentally getting close to the truth), wrote in *New Theatre,* "His is the method of realistic symbolism rather than realistic *representation.*" Although Odets was to say years later that the play was based on "my experiences as a boy in the Bronx," that the characters were people he knew, that it was not "invented," but "felt, remembered, celebrated," very few of the reviewers took the characters as simple human portraits. They were identified as stock characters—usually pejoratively. Yet, although presumably unreal, they were accused of being mad (following Clara's "My whole family's crazy, except Julie"), too abnormal a collection to be a realistic representation of the middle class. What emerges from the contradictions within the reviews is a reluctant and rather pained recognition of what Odets is up to in *Paradise Lost*. The Gordons are a collection of types, most of them with idiosyncrasies (Ben's false good humor, Gus's disconnected thoughts, Katz's anger) which an actor could use as a starting point for turning a type into a character. The critical reaction to the play and Clurman's own comments on the conception of May ("the most stylized figure of all") suggest an overstatement in performance that is not implicit in the script. Some of the characters are specifically identified with a societal counterpart (Julie says, "I feel like a weak market"), but for the most part the identifications are not that direct. They are reflections of familiar attitudes or middle-class values, each with his own disease, his own weakness, and altogether they represent that class in decay.

Leo is a somewhat idealized version of the small businessman,° the best of the middle class—intellectual (his books) and artistic (he designs the handbags that Katz sells). Clara, as wife and mother, is at once protective (she does the abusing, of Katz, of Foley) and self-indulgent (she goes to play cards with the girls when Julie wants her to stay home); her tag-line, "Take a piece of fruit," is at once an invitation and a weapon (she uses it to shut up Gus, to placate Julie). Each of the Gordon children represents a virtue—physical prowess, financial acumen, artistic talent—celebrated by middle-class parents, although the virtues have lost their power. Ben, the Olympic runner with the weak heart, is a familiar American figure, the athletic hero who never finds in later life a triumph to equal his youthful success (see

---

°In his poem on *Lost*, "*Brief an den Stükeschreiber* Odets," an astonished Bertolt Brecht asks, "do you wish to feel sympathy for them?"

Death of a Salesman, or Harold Lloyd's last movie, *Mad Wednesday);* his statue, which stands out prominently in the set, as the publicity photographs indicate, is a totem (how often characters touch it, speak to it; "How like a god!" whispers Gus) which has lost its magic. Julie is a bank clerk who plays the market on paper, imagining success while he dies of sleeping sickness. Pearl is a pianist with no opportunity to perform (she provides the offstage music) and a girl with no chance of happiness (her *Felix* leaves her). Sex (love) is a constant failure here, not only for Pearl, who does not get it, but for those who do. Ben's marriage to Libby (a brassy materialist figure with a fondness for the movies) is a failure, and Kewpie, who buys Libby, discovers that she is not what he really wants. Katz, who fails as a businessman also fails sexually, proves impotent (Gus's joke about "a woman who sleeps with cats" becomes ironic here), and the childless Mrs. Katz becomes a mother to her husband. In his introduction to the play Clurman sees Katz as a "symbol of a capitalism that is incapable for all its 'good will' and intense energy to master its own contradictions," a very genteel way of saying that from the play's point of view capitalism just can not get it up. The Myron-like Gus, garrulous and nostalgic ("I guess failure's gone to my head"); Pike, the ineffectual radical (Odets explained in his letter to Watts that Pike "is no Left-Winger," but a muddled voice of protest); Kewpie, the gangster—these round out the Gordon family circle. The other characters—Phil Foley, the shop delegation, May, the two homeless men—are little more than devices to underline the meaning of the Gordons.

The movement of the play is downward, except for the abrupt upward tilt of Leo's last speech. In Act I, we meet the Gordons and their circle, learn their symbolic defects and their realistic situation; the meeting with the shop delegation establishes that the handbag factory is in trouble. In Act II, eighteen months later, Katz is revealed (as embezzler, as impotent husband) and Ben dies, cut down by police bullets, an apparent suicide; Leo refuses to burn down the business for the insurance—turns down his gangster as Ben does not turn down Kewpie—and the business is doomed. In Act III, "a year and some months later," the house is gone, the Gordons are about to be moved into the street. "One of the objective functions of depression is the expropriation of the owners of small property," wrote Lewis Corey in *The Crisis of the Middle Class*. Paul, the articulate one of the homeless men in Act III, says the same thing differently: "You have been took like a bulldog takes a pussy cat!"

Before the play opened, Odets told an interviewer that *Lost* was the most optimistic play he had written to date: "It's my hope that when people see it they are going to be glad they are alive." For that hope to be fulfilled, the audience would have to believe the final speech of the play, the "red plume in its tail feathers," as Richard Lockridge called it. There are three questions that need to be asked about that last speech: what does it mean? could Leo have made it? is it the proper end of this play? The meaning cannot be found in looking at the words alone. It lies in the total political context and in the rejections that have been made within the play. I do not want to suggest that Odets actually used Lewis Corey's book, although he cited it later, but the ideas to which Corey gave a formal setting were in the political air that Odets breathed. "As the defenses of the middle class are swept away by the whirlwinds of economic disaster, it is driven to action," Corey wrote. "What shall that action be?" Brecht, already a refugee from Germany, living in "my Danish Siberia," simply assumed that the middle class would move to fascism; writing to V. J. Jerome in February 1936, after his return from the United States, he criticized *Lost* vigorously and urged "a broad discussion of the question," that is, that the middle-class sentimentalizers be kept in line. The American Left was less convinced of the inevitability of fascism; the middle class might after all, see the proletarian light. Even *The Communist Manifesto*, which generally saw the middle class as reactionary, said that they could be revolutionary if "they desert their own standpoint to place themselves at that of the proletariat." An unsigned editorial in the *New Masses* which bore the title of Corey's book made this plea: "You need only to know yourselves to know that your place is by the side of the workers, aiding them, following them, fighting in their ranks for the common objective: the right to live and to be happy." "Dare to understand—" cried Corey at the end of his book, echoing a phrase that he had used earlier, "forward, not backward!" Odets

97

told Robert Garland that the play was about "the curious not seeing and accepting of reality," but if it moves to a positive ending it must reach the point of "to know yourselves," of "to understand." Michael Gold wrote that "the bankrupt hero accepts the bankruptcy of capitalism (in symbolic speech), and looks forward to a new life and a better world." Two Leftist reviewers who did not like the play, who suspected its dialectic, were even blunter in their description of that last speech. Clara Bagley, in the *Sunday Worker*, said "the defeatist turned Communist" and James T. Farrell described the speech as "translating into bad poetry Engels' conception of the ascent of man from the kingdom of necessity to the kingdom of freedom."

The radical content of the speech does not depend finally on the climate of ideas which produced it or the labels hung on it by the Right or Left. Within the play capitalism—from Leo's handbags to Kewpie's jobs to the stock market—fails, either dramatically or symbolically. So, too, the rest of the middle-class values. This is indicated by the use of Phil Foley. Not realistic at all (what politician would fail to know and use an Olympic winner in his district?), he is simply a bumptious Irish comic with a tight-lipped partner, who bursts into Act I with his talk of acid and alkaline,° offering a bogus remedy for a wrongly-diagnosed ailment; when he returns in Act III with his *"prosperity* block party," he is still lost in symptoms and impossible cures, although the ills are economic. When Gus suggests that a new administration might solve something, Pike snaps, "Don't be no medium-sized rabbit, Gus." So when Leo finally speaks, dismissing the past, embracing the future, trumpeting "and no *man fights alone!"* it is presumably as much a metaphorical call to revolution as the "STRIKE!" at the end of *Lefty*. If it is not, then it is only a vague positive cry, not that different from Grandpa Vanderhof's prayer at the end of the Moss Hart-George S. Kaufman *You Can't Take It with You* (1936). For that, there would be no need—in fact, no possibility—of all the symbolic rejections.

°This is another indication of the way Odets used popular material. Acid-alkaline chatter was in the air. See, for instance, "Build Your Alkaline Reserve for Health," *Pictorial Review*, November 1934.

Could Leo have made the speech? There are reasons to doubt it. He is capable of decision, of action. We see this, comically, in the opening scene of the play when he rejects the German canary bird. We see it, more seriously, when he accepts the workers' demands and rejects the proposed fire. Perhaps the positive possibilities implicit in these acts are to be understood as operative in an ideational situation. If he can be made to see that his paradise is lost, he may be able to take the next step and see it as well lost. Most of the play is built on questions ("But what is to be done?" "what is happening here?" "Why did we wait so long to know? ") that are answered only by implication. "Don't show it to me," Leo says when Pike offers him the sketch he made of dead men on the garbage dump; the suggestion is that Leo willfully refuses to see. As for "what is to be done," even Pike, after his most extended and violent speech, collapses under Leo's question, "I don't know . . . I mean I don't know . . ." Although Leo is occasionally forceful in small ways, the general impression is that he is unwilling to see what is happening and incapable of dealing with the situation (he gets a nosebleed at one moment of crisis). Harold Clurman explained in his *New Theatre* article that Leo, as he was played, "rarely completes any movement" in the early part of the play and that "Only in the end do we establish a stronger tone for him—something to suggest that now at last he may become an integrated person." This is a sensible director's device for solving a problem in the script, for there is surely nothing in Leo as we know him or in Paul's big accusatory scene to lead to Leo's "No!"—his rejection of Paul's apparent acceptance of defeat and his hortatory step into the future.

Ralph, in *Awake and Sing!*, has some of Leo's problems as a character, but there are other elements in the play that carry it successfully to its positive ending. Are there similar elements in operation here or is it a case, as Clara Bagley said, of Leo's conversion coming "because it is eleven o'clock and the curtain must come down"? The most ingenious argument in favor of the ending can be found in Kenneth Burke's review of the published play. He found three images of destruction in the play—ice, fire, decay—and decided that the first two are rejected, the third accepted and that, out of the decay, "Leo's prophecy of rebirth sprouts." The argument is not convincing, primarily because the images, often taken out of context, do not work together as Burke thought they did. The review is valuable chiefly because it recognized that Odets is not a simple-minded artist (as many of the reviewers suggested after *Lost*) and that Pike is intended as a guide character for Leo (like Jacob for Ralph). I can find no underlying pattern in *Lost* beyond the decline I described above. It is apparent not only in the worsening situation of the Gordons, but in symbolic ways—obviously in Julie's increasing illness, less obviously in Gus's motorcycle, which is a triumphant chariot for Ben and Libby in Act I and can be seen on stage in Act III with one wheel missing. There is nothing to counteract the declension, no parallel action—like the elopment of Hennie and Moe—off which Leo's conversion can feed. Gus's selling his stamp collection, which may have been intended as supportive, is ineffective (despite his nice strutting bit with Foley) because Gus's stamps are never dramatically established. As for the rhetorical pleasure I described in Chapter IV, it is much less likely to work with tired, middle-aged Leo than with youthful Ralph; nor is Clara's final kiss the emotional equivalent of Moe's "I wouldn't trade. . . ." Although Odets has a need to be both positive and negative, as Heywood Broun pointed out in his review, I think the playwright meant the last musical fanfare to be accepted as a triumphant accompaniment to Leo's speech. I cannot help remembering that it comes from the band outside, helping Phil Foley celebrate *prosperity*.

Despite the ending and a few touches (Julia's last scene, Katz's sexual revelations, Pike's denunciatory speeches) which could become ludicrous if not treated gingerly, *Paradise Lost* is almost as "velvety" as Odets thought it was. Of all the Odets plays, it is probably the one that has most to gain from a revival. Now that we are not so enamored of theatrical realism and not so worried about effects without plot-made causes, it might be possible to stage *Lost* to bring out the intricacies, the theatrical life, the comedy and pain with which the family scenes are so rich.

VII. *"Clifford doesn't belong to that crowd"*

WHEN THOMAS SUGRUE asked Clifford Odets the direct question, "Are you a Communist?" the playwright answered, "I am against war. I am against Fascism. I am for a third party." There is a certain charm in that answer, the swagger of the new celebrity using words like semaphore flags, signalling to any of the *American Magazine* readers who knew the code, the conjunction of *war* and *Fascism*—saying *yes* or *my sympathies are there.* In answer to other direct questions in a much less attractive time, Odets told the House Un-American Activities Committee that he had, indeed, been a member of the Communist Party: "My best guess on that would be from toward the end of 1934 to the middle of 1935, covering maybe anywhere from 6 to 8 months." Elia Kazan, listing the members of his unit for the HUAC, said of Odets, "He has assured me that he got out about the same time I did"; Kazan gave late winter or early spring 1936 as the date for his leaving the Party. By 1952, the public hearings were little more than confessionals, ways of clearing one's name if not one's conscience, necessary rituals that had to be performed before absolution—removal from the blacklist—could be given; the HUAC, intent on its own imperfect mosaic of evidence, listened only for the repentant voice and naming of names—certainly not for inconsistencies. Not that the exact date that Odets left the Party matters much. There was no formal break, no public statement, no shattering revelation. He apparently simply drifted away—and not very far, at that; there was no alienation from old associates, old comrades. Such a drift would not even have been against the interests of a Party which was moving into the Popular Front period, shopping as much for big name fellow travelers as for Party regulars.

The date is interesting only because Odets told the HUAC that he left the Party because he was in "the cultural front" and came to distrust "these people . . . as literary or theater critics." If "fantastically bad notices" sent Odets out of the Party, it would be useful to know whether it was before or after the production of *Paradise Lost.* The reception of *Waiting for Lefty* had, of course, been enthusiastic, although, even amid the applause, a reviewer like Stanley Burnshaw could point to minor flaws. With *Awake and Sing!*—almost middle class after *Lefty*—a withdrawal could have been expected. The reaction ranged from Nathaniel Buchwald's "an unimportant play" in the *Daily Worker* to the more tempered objections of Michael Blankfort in *New Masses* and Mary Virginia Farmer in *New Theatre.* Odets's old friend Abner Biberman wrote to *New Masses* protesting Blankfort's review, and got a lecture in reply:

> Proletarian literature is any creative, original and profound writing which furthers the revolutionary interests and the historical mission of the international working class. In other words, proletarian literature is propaganda . . . on behalf of the proletariat.

Obviously, for Blankfort, *Awake* did not fit that definition. James T. Farrell wrote a long, complicated letter to *New Theatre* defending *Awake* as superior revolutionary literature.

Blankfort and Farrell reversed roles for *Lost.* Blankfort wrote a generally favorable review in the *Daily Worker* (December 13, 1935) and Farrell demolished the play in *Partisan Review and Anvil* (February 1936). Jay Gerlando in the *Daily Worker* (February 7, 1936), picking up Blankfort's one criticism of the play, that the Gordons were too abnormal, came down heavier on *Lost,* and Clara Bagley in the *Sunday Worker* (February 16, 1936) simply dismissed it as a bad play and "bad Marxism." *New*

Masses (December 24, 1935) carried a very enthusiastic review by Robert Forsythe (Kyle Crichton), but Stanley Burnshaw turned up later (February 11, 1936) with "An Obituary," which attacked Odets's Marxism. Playing the nuances, one might suspect that the initial *Lost* reviews were better than the *Awake* reviews because the Popular Front had become official between the two openings; and that something (his departure from the Party?) happened between December and February to call Odets's Marxism in question. That impression is heightened by a remark in Gerlando's article: "Marxists have often been accused of making rules for the writer, of throwing cold water on his imagination, but these are silly accusations that come only from ignorance." The neatness of my assumption is somewhat disturbed by the fact that Michael Gold, the good old Party hack, came riding to Odets's defense *(New Masses,* February 18, 1936), but then his remarks on Odets's play were really only ammunition in his attack on Farrell, the first gun in the battle that would take place later that year with the publication of Farrell's *A Note on Literary Criticism,* in which he continued his attempt to teach dialectic materialism to the Party regulars.

Although Earl Browder told the American Writers' Congress in 1935 that "There is no fixed 'Party line' by which works of art can be automatically separated into sheep and goats" (as he later told Daniel Aaron that Party functionaries were never really that concerned with what writers said), it is obvious that the Communist critics did not hesitate to tell Odets what he should have done and that their *should* tended to wobble in the ideational wind. Michael Blankfort told the HUAC that he did not really know whether or not the Party had a line on the Odets plays, but that after his reviews of *Awake* and *Lost,* his review tickets were stopped, first at *New Masses,* and then at *Daily Worker.* Of course, there may have been fewer public pressures on Odets. He told the HUAC that the criticisms of *Lefty* warned him against "left tendencies . . . which in those days meant that one had better be careful not to be a Trotskyite," but I cannot find those warnings in the reviews I have read. According to Kazan, V. J. Jerome was one of the officials assigned to pass the Party line to his unit, but Bertolt Brecht's letter to Jerome suggested that the job was not too well done—if

Lost were an example. "And so I persisted in going along my own line and saying and writing what did come out of my true center," Odets told the hearings.

In the summer of 1935, still in the Party, Clifford Odets had his one adventure as an active revolutionist, the investigatory trip to Cuba which is itself a sad, funny comment on the times and on the use and abuse of the American artist. There was something genuine to investigate. The hopes that followed the overthrow of Gerardo Machado's dictatorship in 1933, that flickered during the presidency of Ramón Grau San Martin, were dampened when Washington refused to recognize Grau's government and then smothered completely when he was ousted by Fulgencio Batista in January 1934. By 1935, Batista and his president, Carlos Mendieta, had settled into a dictatorship of their own, solidified when the general strike in March of that year was forcefully put down. At the American Writers' Congress in April, Lola de la Torriente reported that two of the selected delegates were in prison (as were a great many intellectuals and students) and urged, "I hope the League of American Writers you are about to form will send a representative with the delegation that is shortly to go to Cuba to investigate the actual conditions under which the people of Cuba are living." When the American Commission to Investigate Labor and Social Conditions in Cuba set sail on the *Oriente* (the kind of tourist ship that Hennie and Moe would have taken) on June 29, the League's representative, Odets (the biggest name on the commission), was titular chairman. The members represented a variety of groups, many of them fronts, and were identified by the press as everything from "Liberals" (Philadelphia *Bulletin*, July 3) to "a squad of east-side communists" (the nervously anti-Red *National Republic*, August 1). The *Bulletin* quoted Odets's father: "Clifford doesn't belong to that crowd."

Once they were aboard and tactical discussion began, Odets later told the HUAC, he discovered that the real head of the group was Conrad Komorowski, who he assumed was a Communist because he was so professional at his work, and that they were going not to investigate but to be arrested. The delegation was isolated from the regular tourists when the boat arrived in

Havana, marched to Tiscornia detention camp, kept overnight, marched back the next night and shipped off to New York. It was almost certainly uncomfortable and it was probably frightening (Odets later made much of the menacing guards with submachine guns), but it was also opéra bouffe. Odets himself described the attempt to get rid of letters when the police came aboard as "like a scene from a Charlie Chaplin movie." If publicity was the object, the trip was a success. There were protests, telegrams to Cordell Hull, a meeting at the Longacre Theatre with the Group's William Challee in the chair. The heroes were welcomed at the pier on July 6 by a spontaneous gathering (the *Daily Worker* had been plugging their arrival for two days) which numbered from 150 (New York *Daily News*, July 7) to more than 600 "workers and professionals" (*Daily Worker*, July 8), to whom Odets spoke briefly. "Caffrey has a heart of sugar," he is supposed to have said, a probable statement since, from his point of view, the real villains in the piece were the U.S. State Department, Ambassador Jefferson Caffrey and the American sugar interests. It is less likely, politically and personally, that he said of a guard who used the word *scram*, as the New York *Journal* reported, "Imagine a slanty-eyed Latin using that expression. Those greasy people who use a knife to eat peas—they don't know what existence means." Odets's own accounts of the trip appeared in a wireless story sent to the New York *Post* from the returning *Oriente*, an article in the *New Masses*, and his contribution ("Machine Gun Reception") to the pamphlet *Rifle Rule in Cuba* (Carleton Beals, who regularly reported from Latin America, had a condemnatory piece on United States-Cuba relations) published by the Provisional Committee for Cuba in September. Except for the publication of the pamphlet, the whole affair pretty much died out after a final protest rally on July 10 at which Odets shared the platform with Beals and Roger Baldwin. The whole incident was forgotten—probably even by Odets once he had written *The Cuban Play* (1938) and failed to get it produced—until the HUAC resurrected it in 1952.

Odets's other political activities in the months after his first success had more to do with his profession as a playwright. Even the confrontation with Pirandello is a theatrical anecdote of sorts. When the Italian dramatist arrived in New York, "a bright Fascist badge in his lapel, a fat Hollywood contract in his pocket" *(New Theatre,* August 1935), a delegation of writers, Odets and John Howard Lawson among them, called on him in his stateroom on July 23 to protest his support of Mussolini and the Ethiopian invasion. A comedy of cross-purpose ensued in which Pirandello had to be disabused of the notion that he was being honored by a delegation of fellow artists and, as the New York *Times* reported, "The 'conference' broke up with some rancor." Pirandello persisted in his contention that art and politics were separate, and *New Theatre* urged its readers to send their protests to him at the Waldorf. The *World-Telegram* reported that Pirandello had been scheduled to attend a performance of *Awake and Sing!* on July 22, flanked by LaGuardia and Odets, but that he had cried off because he "was too weary to stir," but the story, if true, does not—as the *World-Telegram* implied— explain the delegation. The year 1935 is explanation enough.

More central to Odets's concerns were the two plays that he wrote for special performances during 1935, for this was the year that saw not four but six Odets plays in production. For Morris Carnovsky, Odets wrote the monologue, *I Can't Sleep,* which Gerald Rabkin has correctly described as "a party play in that it overtly considers the greatest of revolutionary sins, heresy." After passing a silent beggar by, the speaking character returns and offers him money which he refuses (a preview of the end of *Paradise Lost?),* an incident which unleashes a flow of words. Blitzstein at first talks in private terms about his isolation from his family, but, as the revelation unfolds, we discover that he is a worker who has turned his back on his class, a renegade Marxist who has to hide in the subway to keep from hearing the accusing music of the May Day parade. "Look in my face, comrade. Look at me, look, look, look!!!" Carnovsky performed the piece on May 19 at the Mecca Temple and again on May 26 at a "Gala Theatre Night" for the New Theatre League; the play was published in *New Theatre* (February 1936). For the Negro People's Theatre, for whom William Challee had earlier directed a production of *Waiting for Lefty,* Odets wrote *Remember,* which Herbert Rappaport called a play "of the horrors of 'relief,'" showing "the fallacy of resignation." Odets is supposed to have directed the play for its October 19 performance at the Manhattan Opera House, but the program for a later production (October 26) says that it was "Collectively staged and directed by cast." For the rest, there were articles on revolutionary theatre (*New Theatre*, January 1936; *Controversy*, February 1936); speeches on the same subject (a banquet for the *New Theatre* staff, October 3, 1935); service as a judge in a "relief" play contest (announced *New Theatre*, January 1936); an offer of free advice, during rehearsals, on any "valuable" first-run play (a personal ad in *New Masses*, November 19, 1935).

Such a list suggests the extent and the immediacy of Odets's involvement with the political and cultural scene in the year of his first success. In the years that followed, he continued to serve on committees, sign petitions, make donations (as the HUAC pointed out at length), often for good if Party-supported causes. As he said to the investigating committee, "the lines of leftism, liberalism, in all of their shades and degrees, are constantly crossing like a jangled chord on a piano." His image simply as a good liberal is slightly muddied by a tendency to bend with the line of the Party even after he had left it; the pacifism in *Night Music* (1940) is colored by the fact that the Soviet-Nazi pact dictated that the Communists call for non-intervention at that time. The one touching moment in the HUAC hearings, a confused and garrulous two days that is almost as much to Odets's discredit as to the Committee's, came when Odets, having put the Communists behind him, said, "If I may say so, the foolish position of a man like myself is that he has no party to belong to."

In the complicated history of the relationship between the American intellectual and the Communist Party in the 1930s, Odets is little more than a footnote (Daniel Aaron gave him a few paragraphs), but I have devoted much space to the subject both because his success in 1935 was a reflection of the atmosphere in which the relationship flourished and because his own political allegiance so clearly affected his plays. *Waiting for Lefty* and *Till the Day I Die* were explicitly Communist; the endings of both *Awake and Sing!* and *Paradise Lost* were revolutionary—at least, by implication. Odets's commitment to

Marxism was more emotional than intellectual and it continued far beyond his presumed formal break with the Communist Party; as Gerald Rabkin pointed out in *Drama and Commitment*, it provided him with the redemption metaphor that was the spine of all his plays in the 1930s. If, as Rabkin suggested, he lost both belief and metaphor in later years, the impulse that pulled him to the party, that made him regret his "foolish position," kept him from succumbing completely to that other self so attracted to success and its physical accoutrements. Odets was, after all, more than political man.

Line by line, there are probably more factual errors in the pages on the leftist theatre in Murray Kempton's *Part of Our Time* than in any similar commentary on the period. Yet, there is insight as well:

> Loyal as they were to the revolution, they were just as loyal to the traditions of the theater. When they had their pictures taken for their programs, they took off their glasses and combed their hair and had themselves photographed soft focus.

This comment on the leftist playwrights as a group is certainly true of Odets. It might be placed alongside a line from John McCarten: "Even though he likes to carry five-hundred dollar bills around in his pocket and lives in a penthouse, he is unfailingly interested in the plight of the masses." Lurking behind the journalistic put-down in both these statements is the truth that Odets, the radical playwright, was also Odets, the child of show business. After *Paradise Lost* failed, the latter packed the former and headed west.

VIII. *"Odets, Where Is Thy Sting?"*

O N THE BACK PAGE of the first issue of *The Flying Grouse*, the Group Theatre magazine that never lasted beyond its second issue, there is a photograph labeled, "AFTER PARADISE LOST—A Bon Voyage to Clifford Odets after the show." At the center of this gathering of the cast and their guests is a figure dressed in an overcoat as if ready to depart—the only person seated on a chair and, caught between the floor-sitters and the standers, the obvious focus for the reader's eye. At first glance, one supposes it is Odets, about to be launched, but *no*—Odets, arms crossed, smiling slightly, looking directly at the camera, is to one side of the first standing row. Elia Kazan's left hand rests lightly on his shoulder. I cannot imagine that Marion Post, who took the picture, was going for symbolic prescience, but, for me, the picture is a much more appropriate introduction to Odets in Hollywood than a more conventional celebrity send-off photograph could ever be. Until he moved to California in the 1940s, after the death of the Group, Odets was constantly pulled back to New York, to his place in that photograph. "Lucky to have people like the Group to come back to—" he told a New York *Herald Tribune* interviewer when he returned east after his first movie, "people who understand what I'm working at and trying to do."

The seven pictures that bear Odets's name as writer or director are not a true indication of the amount of work he did in Hollywood. Shortly before his death he told Michael J. Mendelsohn, "I suppose that by now I've written—written or rewritten secretly for some friends of mine—fifteen or eighteen, close to twenty films." Before he ever went to Hollywood, he told Richard Watts Jr. that there were only three things that could keep a theater person from going to Hollywood: "Money, one; a viewpoint, an ideal, an idea which shouts inside him for constant and multiformed stage expression, two; self-recognition of steady and progressive improvement in his work both as craftsman and artist, three." Since he never had the first and was attracted to it ("I'm crazy about money," he told the Philadelphia *Record*), there was a continuing struggle between his art and his well-being. This is what Harold Clurman meant when he wrote in *The Fervent Years*, "For Odets . . . Hollywood was Sin." Clurman later recalled that he laughed when he quoted the line to Odets, only to get this rebuke, "What are you laughing about? It is." Yet, it is not quite that simple, not merely a matter of the conflict between fleshpots and poet's attic, because the film, too, is an art form. Odets always distrusted the Hollywood product and its influence on people (see Jacob's speeches in *Awake and Sing!*, Joe's in *Clash by Night*) and insisted that he wanted no part of it: "But I won't be a party to the fraud the screen has been perpetrating on the public for years. Boy gets girl. Life is swell." Yet the technical quality, the size of the audience, the possibility of saying something significant, socially or artistically—these always attracted him. Beginning with his first trip to Hollywood, he offered interviews praising and blaming the industry, the relative weight of praise or blame depending on whether he was arriving or leaving, beginning a new film that interested him or running home to the stage. There is a large helping of rationalization in all those interviews, but there is truth too. Ironically, the first of the interviews denouncing Hollywood for its fraudulency was part of a publicity campaign; it can be found in the Press Book that Paramount prepared for Odets's first film, *The General Died at Dawn* (1936).

Speculation about when and for how much Clifford Odets would go to Hollywood began shortly after the opening of

Awake and Sing! "There lives a young man in our town who, if he and Hollywood don't look out, is in danger of becoming a foremost dramatist," wrote Gilbert W. Gabriel in his review of *Awake.* A few days later, George Ross reported that Odets had been offered $500 a week after *Waiting for Lefty* opened and that the bid had gone to $1250 with the arrival of *Awake.* Clurman said in *The Fervent Years* that MGM was willing to go to $3000 at one point, which is believable when one remembers that most of the financing of *Paradise Lost* came from that studio ("for reasons entirely mysterious to me," Clurman wrote). The Odets market dropped after the reviews of *Lost.* The playwright went to Hollywood anyway, ostensibly to look around, but, by the time Sidney Skolsky wrote his column for February 25, 1936, Odets was in Lake Arrowhead "working on his flicker with Director Lewis Milestone." The closing price was $20,000 for eight-weeks work. Heady figures for 1935. Back in New York after eleven (rather than eight) weeks, he told the *Herald Tribune,* "Why, that will underwrite my work here for a full two years." He was back in Hollywood before the year was out.

Paramount, as the Press Book indicates, peddled *The General Died at Dawn* as an "adventure-romance," which it was, stressing its stars (Gary Cooper and Madeleine Carroll) and its story. Yet, one of the selling points was Odets ("A Name Author") and an incidental emphasis can be found in phrases like "the oppressed peasants" and "awakening of China's teeming millions" scattered through the promotion material. A fairly conventional melodrama, based on a story by Charles G. Booth, the movie tells how the wicked General Yang ("A certain honorable tootsie roll . . ." says the hero. "A head-breaker, a heart-breaker, a strike-breaker! Altogether a four-star rat!") is overthrown by an American name O'Hara ("You ask me why I'm for oppressed people? Because I got a background of oppression myself, and O'Hara's and elephants don't forget. What's better work for an American than helping fight for democracy?") who educates and wins his lovely Judy in the process. As the quotations suggest, there is at least a hint of the political Odets in the dialogue. Even a hint is a surprise if one believes Lewis Milestone's account of the difficulties he and Odets faced on the film. After William LeBaron, the producer, accepted Odets's second script

111

the censorship department had moved in. A real Chinese general stalked the Paramount lot with official frowns. . . . For a time it became a free-for-all in which any one from the Chinese consulate had the right to write a scene, and anyone from the censorship board had a right to suggest new lines and situations.

"They hired me on the basis of writing talent," Odets told the *Herald Tribune*, "but they fine-tooth-combed the script, for traces of radicalism, I suppose." When the movie was released in September, Frank S. Nugent headed his Sunday piece "Odets, Where Is Thy Sting?"° Nugent, very snottily, described the "claque," the Odets enthusiasts who came to see their hero's first film and clapped noisily at every possible social-conscience line until they could find no more to respond to: "They had enjoyed an incendiary ten minutes and the fires of class philosophy burned out. The picture continued—it had never been anything else—as a straightforward melodrama." For the most part, the other New York reviewers, probably responding to Odets's name, treated *General* as a standard movie of its type, noting only that it had socially significant overtones. Only Sidney Kaufman in *New Masses* and Robert Stebbins in *New Theatre* treated the film as an attempt to transform a popular genre, to, in Stebbins's words, "use the thriller to convey some unpalatable truths." In his pre-release article, which contained two scenes drawn from the shooting script, Kaufman said, "this melodramatic yarn rings like a coin from the nickelodeon mint—but, godalmighty, what a different face it wears." There seems to be a deal of wishful thinking in operation in the two reviews. The film, as Odets said years later, was "full of good ideas, but in the

---

°For the sake of history, let me record that Nugent's now famous pun was first used—publicly, at least—by John Anderson in his review of *Waiting for Lefty* in the New York *Journal*, February 11, 1935: " 'Comes de Rewolution' we need not ask, to paraphrase several gags, 'Odets, where is thy sting?' " A few days later, February 20, Walter Winchell played a variation on the line in his review of *Awake and Sing!* in the New York *Mirror:* "Odets—there is thy sting." *Sic transit gloria* note: Chauncey Howell, reviewing the 1966 revival of *The Country Girl* for *Women's Wear Daily*, September 30, credited the ancient wheeze to Kenneth Tynan, who was a child of seven when Anderson and Winchell wished the joke on the world.

end it was a set of clichés on which we made some good birth-day decorations."

If Odets, the radical playwright, was barely visible in the *General,* he was in evidence—although not quite seriously—in Hollywood itself. Walter Winchell's probably apocryphal anec-dote gives the feel of a number of stories coming out of Holly-wood at the time. Moss Hart, meeting Odets at a party, men-tioned that Odets had made many scenario writers turn Com-munist. " 'You mean,' he asked, 'my plays converted them?' 'No,' said Hart, 'your salary.' " Almost as frivolous is Harold Clurman's report in *The Fervent Years* in which Odets comes across as a self-appointed boy conspirator in the labor troubles surrounding the attempt of the Screen Writers' Guild to win a Guild shop and a minimum basic agreement: "Odets, annoyed and flattered, whispered to me that at MGM he was thought to be the source of all the trouble." In all the news stories that came out of Hollywood during the Guild's losing April-to-August battle and in the 1937 and 1938 follow-ups, there is no mention of Odets. Perhaps he was not talking about taxi strikes alone when he told the House Un-American Activi-ties Committee "I have never been near a strike in my life." He was, after all, a commuter.

He wrote two other scripts close on the heels of *General: Get-tysburg,* which was not filmed at all, and *Castles in Spain,* which was also known as *The River is Blue.* The latter provides an in-teresting insight into both Hollywood and Odets's career as a screen writer. According to John Howard Lawson, Lewis Mile-stone had always wanted to film an Ilya Ehrenburg novel, and when, after *General* was released, Walter Wanger approached him and Odets to do a movie, the director suggested that *The Love of Jeanne Ney* might be successfuly adapted to a Spanish Civil War background. By the end of 1936, according to the New York *Times,* Odets had a "preliminary scenario" finished. "It was an inept melodrama," wrote Lawson, "bearing no re-semblance to the novel and having no bearing on the events in Europe." The harshness of that judgment may stem in part from the fact that when it was written Lawson (one of the Hollywood Ten) had been to jail for refusing to testify before the HUAC and Odets had been what is called a "friendly witness." In fact,

113

Odets did use Ehrenburg, as the two scripts of *Castles* in the Theatre Collection of the New York Public Library indicate. Marco shoots Norma's father, as Andrew does Jeanne's; the art dealer's daughter is blind as is Jeanne's cousin with whom she comes to live in Paris. I suspect that the grossness of the wedding dinner in Odets's script, somewhat wrong in tone for the art dealer as he has been drawn (his name is Ney), stems from the New Year's Eve Party in Ehrenburg's novel. These are incidental likenesses, of course, evidence of the script's original source but not of a genuine attempt to adapt the novel to the screen. One might make a case for the central plot's being a variation on the Ehrenburg book. As Jeanne learns from Andrew's death that her love is the "cause" and returns to Russia, so Norma learns that her love is inescapably bound to the "cause" (Marco: "Life is only one way for you—with *me*—to Spain!") and returns, singing, to Spain. Yet, this is the story Odets told in *Awake* and *Lost*, the conversion of a passive person to an active commitment, the choice of life (the war in Spain) over death (the Ney household). The explicit social comment lies in the scenes of fighting, refugees, and hunger that are juxtaposed to the personal story. The weakness of the script is that it splits in two, that the Paris section is so obviously Norma's sentimental story with not only Spain but Marco pushed off the screen. Lawson was brought in to rewrite the script in 1937 and the film, directed by William Dieterle, was released as *Blockade*, in 1938. Lawson's script was, at once, more Hollywood and more propagandistic than Odets's had been. He used the corniest kind of spy story (Norma's connection with the bad guys might have come from *The General Died at Dawn*), but a direct appeal to the audience—Henry Fonda's face in huge close-up: "Stop the murder of innocent people! The world can stop it! Where's the conscience of the world?" A final compromise: the war and the participants were never identified. To Odets's credit he had tried to dramatize the Spanish Civil War as early as 1936 and he had tried to write a script with some human substance amid its sentimental bromides.

"And so Luise Rainer and Clifford Odets were married—" began "The Romantic Story of Luise Rainer's Surprise Marriage" in *Photoplay,* and the same author, Leonard Hall, in a supposedly comic article for the New York *Journal,* made much of the fact that the proletarian playwright had come to Hollywood and carried off the ultimate American prize, a movie star. To the ordinary American (the circulation of *Photoplay* was a great deal larger than that of *New Masses),* the real triumph of Odets was not *Waiting for Lefty* but his marriage to Luise Rainer. She was not just any movie star, but the toast of the moment, the Viennese beauty who, when the marriage took place, had already won an Academy Award for *The Great Ziegfeld* (1936) and finished filming *The Good Earth,* for which she would win another. When Odets first came to Hollywood, Miss Rainer later told Louella Parsons, the playwright, having seen her in *Escapade,* asked to be introduced to her. They immediately disliked each other: "It was as if we sensed a great tragedy might come to us if we fell in love." But fall in love they did and were married, January 8, 1937, quietly, in her Brentwood home. "They were castaways in Hollywood . . ." sighed a gaudily written account of the wedding in the New York *Daily News.* That was the tone of the feature stories and the fan-magazine articles, in which Clifford and Luise were two individualists, serious and sensitive artists unhappy in the artificiality of Hollywood. Funnily enough, it was probably half-true although the strain of being sincere and special with a *Modern Screen* reporter watching must have caused a little of the artificiality to rub off. The dream marriage did not last. Mrs. Odets sued for divorce in 1938, charging mental cruelty. "Clifford is a brilliant boy, a genius, perhaps," she told Louella, "but as all people who are so intense and so completely absorbed in their work, difficult to live with." Louella was convinced she still loved him, and indeed, with Louis Nizer as a kind of re-matchmaker, they were reconciled before the year was out. Temporarily. By the time *Six Plays* (1939) was published, the original dedication to *Golden Boy* (1937)—"For Luise, Artist, Wife, Best Friend!"—had been reduced to a simple "For Luise." The divorce took place in May 1940.

IX. *Over My Dead Body*

SHORTLY BEFORE Sheila Barrett opened an engagement at the Rainbow Room in the fall of 1936, there was an item in the New York *Daily News* saying that Clifford Odets had written a skit for her. Aside from the parody material she usually performed, her act contained a character sketch, "Not the Type," about a young actress failing to get work in a casting office. The subject (the echo of "The Young Actor" in *Waiting for Lefty*) and the tone ("pathos and humor" reported the New York *Sun*) suggest Odets, but night club comediennes work without programs and the Odets skit—if it existed—was never identified.

The one new Odets play performed during 1936 was neither new nor Odets. In April of that year, some of the Group actors appeared on the Fleischman Hour in what was billed as an original Odets radio script based on the life of Sarah Bernhardt. It was a variation on a 1934 script by SKOB, a collaborative effort identified by the initials of the four actor-writers involved: Art Smith, Elia Kazan, Clifford Odets, Roman Bohnen. The typescript in the Library of Congress is identified as Episode No. 1 of a radio series to be called *Stage Stars of History* or *Stage Stars of the Past* and holding out the promise of future installments on luminaries such as Irving, Booth, Duse, Mrs. Fiske. The series never materialized. It seems likely that the script was dusted off, perhaps revised (by Odets? he was in Hollywood at the time) when, after the closing of *The Case of Clyde Griffiths,* the Group had a chance to perform again on the program for which they had done a scene from *Awake* a year earlier. The script is an incredibly awful conversion play in which Bernhardt, by flashback (the Michel she sent to death in the Franco-Prussian War) and in the present (her old prompter, dying as they do a scene from *Camille* together), learns the pointlessness of war. It ends with her going off to hearten the boys at the front ("Major, show me the way!") and with a marching song blaring at full. Aaron Stein's description, in which Bernhardt refuses to entertain the troops, suggests that the ending was rewritten to make the play more consistent, but his review gives the impression that it was not improved.

The big Odets play of 1936 was to have been *The Silent Partner.* Even before *Paradise Lost* opened, there was a report that he was "applying the finishing touches to a new play in sixteen scenes." *Partner* has only nine, but the item did not need to be factual to give information. The play was in the making. After he went to Hollywood, reports kept coming out about the play he was working on, then called *Over My Dead Body,* and the promise of fall production. When Harold Clurman read it that summer ("his most ambitious and his most incomplete script" he called it in *The Fervent Years*), he turned it back for revision in the hope that Odets "could imbue these central characters with the life he meant them to have." It was not until 1937 that the play was put into rehearsal, but it never got to the production stage. Since this was one of the moments—after the failure of *Johnny Johnson*—when the Group looked as though it might break down for good, the reasons, personal and professional, for shelving the script were complicated: expense, likelihood of failure, need for further revisions—these were the official ones. "And I was very hurt," Odets said later, "but not intelligent or mature enough to say, 'Stop the shit and do the play. It's necessary for me. And after all the sacrifices I've made, just do the play and lose $40,000. It's worth it to me.' " Necessary, perhaps; important, certainly. It continued to preoccupy him, at least enough to make him work it into interviews and news releases during 1938. "It will be the best labor play ever produced in this country or in any other country," he told John

117

McCarten. When he brought it back to the Group in the summer of 1939, "revised very slightly," Clurman turned it down once again; "the play's mood and the plot pre-dated the progress in legislation of the past five years." One scene was printed in *New Theatre* in March 1937, but the play was never published.

> Its central action was a strike that had been forced upon the workers and in the course of which a variety of figures would be brought together, the backward workers discovering the value of unionism, the prejudiced ones the balm of solidarity, and the misled ones the wisdom of the Communists who, unobtrusively, were among the leaders of the strike. Almost always the strike was lost (a victory might create illusions about the value of mere trade unionism) and sometimes one of its leaders was killed. The shock of defeat, the education through struggle, which then came to a leading character would provide the novel with its political lilt. . . .

This description of the proletarian novel (by Irving Howe and Lewis Coser in *The American Communist Party*) would serve as well for *The Silent Partner,* at least for the version in the Library of Congress (second draft, dated 6/26/36). The appropriateness of the Howe-Coser paragraph suggests that the play is an ideational throwback to *Waiting for Lefty.* The strike has been forced on the workers since their attempts to form a real (as against a company) union has led to dismissals, and in the course of the play the company provokes the violence it wants. Anthony, the unobtrusive Communist, shows his wisdom by voting to call off the strike, to build strength for a future confrontation, but he shows his bravery when, outvoted, he fights alongside his fellow workers. The destruction of the milk, shipped in by sympathizers, converts Mrs. Finch to the strike ("May any man who votes to end our strike burn in hell forever!"), her original opposition to it stemming from weakness presumably, not from tactics as in Anthony's case. Crane, who constantly talks an it-can't-happen-here line, learns that it can ("NOW I KNOW!" is his line and the title of II, 4). The strike is lost and Lovelace, the idealistic (cf. the practical Anthony) leader, is killed. Since this is Odets, there is an interesting death pattern running through the play, from the first scene, a union meeting in a graveyard, through the fine stage image that ends II, 3, the dancing Negro "with a horrible grin on his face" doing "a Dance of Death," to the wake in the Lovelace house (III, 1). It is Lovelace's brother Christie, the juvenile lead, whose education provides the lilt.

"It's the Christies of the world who'll do the work—plant the seed, bring in the harvest," Lovelace says in II, 3. "Myself, I don't feel like a man . . . too much with the head." A remnant of bourgeois culture, Lovelace (like Jacob, like Pike) is a figure through whom the main learning character can reach his awareness. Oddly enough, it includes the rejection of a standard Odets idea—that this is no world to be married in—for Christie and Pearl stand together at the end. "What is the strike for?" asks Pearl. "If it's not for love, what is it for? If it's not to get married, what's it for? If it's not for babies, what's it for?" In his defense of *Rocket to the Moon*, Odets said that he hoped to prove in *Partner* that "love and the urge to strike spring from a very similar origin." It seems obvious that, for all that it conforms to type, *Partner* is a step toward *Rocket*. Lovelace, siding with Pearl against Christie's reluctance, has a line that Mr. Prince will later use to describe Ben Stark: "Most of us live like icebergs—three quarters under water." Even the names (Lovelace's nickname is Lovey) emphasize the new direction that Odets's concern for the good life was taking.

Partner makes use of conventions other than those that Howe and Coser list (for example, the inevitable scene in which the *agent provocateur* is exposed) and the characters never grow beyond the stereotypes from which they start. Its gravest weakness is a crowded final scene, confused in its action and its ideology. Its chief virtues are the cross talk in the workers' gatherings and a bizarre cartoon scene, a meeting of the Law and Order League. "I think you're all vaudeville comedians!" says Gracie (the sympathetic plant president, another victim of the capitalism he serves), and he is right. The platitudinous members of the League, the opaque-mouthed "labor relations counsel" ("and my confrere here will ascertain me") and his quick-tempered gangster associate would not be out of place in Marc Blitzstein's *The Cradle Will Rock* (1937). All the scene needs is judicious cutting and the right kind of music. Odets said later that "five of the nine scenes in it are the best writing I've ever done." He did not say which five, so there is no point in quibbling, except over the number. *The Silent Partner* is interesting for some of the things it attempts, but it is finally a pretty bad play.

The Cuban Play is even worse. It, too, dates from 1936. At least, at that time, Odets was working on a one-act play, *The Law of Flight,* based on the death of Antonio Guiteras. The *Ley de Fuga,* as Carleton Beals explained it in *Rifle Rule in Cuba* ("shot in the back under the pretext that he 'was trying to escape' "), is hardly an exact description of what happened to Guiteras. The Secretary of Interior, War and Navy in the cabinet of Ramón Grau San Martin, Guiteras later formed *Joven Cuba* to fight the Batista government and was killed in pitched battle on May 8, 1935 just as he and his associate, General Carlos Aponte, were about to slip away to the United States. Although the hero of *The Cuban Play* is named Lorca (a conscious choice, honoring Federico Garcia Lorca, who had been killed by the Franco forces in 1936) and the details and characterization are presumably fictional, there are enough parallels (the Grau cabinet post, Young Cuba, an Aponte character, death before embarcation) to indicate that a Guiteras play was still intended. The typescript in the Library of Congress is dated February 1, 1938, but much of the text (the anti-Roosevelt material, the arguments borrowed directly from Beals, an apparent reference to the 1934-35 theater season) suggests that it belongs to an earlier Odets. There was talk of a production in 1938, but it came to nothing; the play was never published.

Like Anthony in *Partner,* Antonio Lorca is a Communist who preaches sense not violence, opposing the General Strike ("Men who agitate now for an abortive strike are traitors to the people, wittingly or otherwise"), arguing against terror tactics. In one scene (II, 10) after Primo calls for terror in a speech that ends as an inside joke ("I have no scruple against rifle rule in Cuba"), Lorca denounces his opponent: "You are a sick romantic infant. You express a way of life essentially romantic, anarchistic and individual. . . . Today terror is counter-revolutionary." The strike does come, as it did historically, and it is crushed. Lorca and General Delgado (Aponte) are ready to go to Mexico to get guns, to carry on the fight, when they and their followers are gunned down by Rojas. This is probably the most negative of Odets's political plays. Lorca's description of the city of his dreams ("call it Avalon"), "a future place of happy people . . . not one hungry face, not one sullen mouth," is two scenes back and is delivered, in any case, at a moment thick with expectation of disaster. To find the conventional lilt in *The Cuban Play,* the audience would have to look to the frame (Lorca's story is a play within a play) in which a Cuban revolutionary comes to persuade an American playwright to write a drama about his suffering country. Yet, the playwright, who appears in brief, narrative scenes during the first two acts, is not even present in Act III, although a note at the head of III, 3 (the Avalon scene) suggests a prefatory scene for him. At the end of the play, however, there is nothing left but the Batista forces with the corrupt Rojas in command and the bodies of Lorca and his friends scattered around the stage. There is no one left—as in *Golden Boy* and *The Big Knife*—to turn the deaths into positive statements.

There is an attempt to complicate Lorca as a character by making Rojas an old school chum of his, an ex-believer who has sold out for "a lewd and lavish life" and thus suggesting a brother-against-brother conflict; by introducing Lorca's sick mother and unhappy sister to show the victimized family who do not understand. But, since we usually see Lorca in debate, he seldom seems more than a mouthpiece. In fact the play is relentlessly full of speeches, explanations of Cuban politics and the economics of sugar imperialism. One suspects that an audience would not last through the long first scene. The most interesting thing about the play is its departure from Odets's customary form, not only in the movement between playwright and subject, but in the use of set satiric scenes (for instance, a tourist agent meeting a ship, a speech to be delivered from the runway, or two American businessmen chatting as the lights of Havana recede). These last and a comic scene in which Delgado teases and robs a paymaster are the most effective bits in an otherwise impossible play.

121

It is probably not fair to judge *The Silent Partner* and *The Cuban Play* too harshly—to let adjectives like "impossible" rise to my typing fingers—since they are obviously not finished scripts. Yet, I do not want to give the impression that there are hidden Odets treasures still unpublished. The two plays are revenants, the sectarian Odets of *Lefty* haunting the author of *The General Died at Dawn*. It is unlikely that Odets could have initiated such scripts after 1936, and it is revelatory of his political uncertainty that, particularly in *The Cuban Play*, he did not cut away references which so obviously reflect Party attitudes dating from 1934–35 that the Popular Front had pretty much put out to pasture by 1938. The intellectual narrowness of the scripts and the concomitant thinness of character is matched by an openness of form, a variousness in scene, an inventiveness in the use of the stage that Odets would not show again until—and then muted—*Night Music* and *Clash by Night*. While he worried with *The Silent Partner* and *The Cuban Play* he was, happily, getting on with *Golden Boy* and *Rocket to the Moon*.

X. *"Whatever you got ina your nature to do isa not foolish!"*

I REALLY WROTE this play to be a hit, to keep the Group Theatre together," Clifford Odets once said of *Golden Boy*. It was a job that needed doing in 1937, for the members of the Group had dispersed after the failure of *Johnny Johnson*, most of them to Hollywood. As Robert Coleman told the story, Luther Adler, who could not stand Hollywood, returned to New York, opened an office and announced that Odets's play (then, still an idea) would be the first Group production that fall. The prodigals began to drift back to New York. Odets came, with the story in outline, and wrote it while the Group actors mounted a twenty-four-hour guard on him to keep him working. In "The Fabulous Fanatics," a *Stage* article on the Group, John Paxton added to the "legend" (Harold Clurman's word in *The Fervent Years*). While Odets was stuck on the third act, Luise Rainer "fussed around her husband in affectionate flurry, got in his hair and the typewriter keys." In desperation, the Group decided to isolate her, gave her an office and a pile of German scripts to read, left her happily at work while Odets finished the play. Like most show-business anecdotes, this one, however fanciful its details, has an inner truth: the Group badly needed a script to pull them back together and Odets needed to concentrate on a play.

The story and the Odets statement that open this chapter

imply that *Golden Boy* is little more than a potboiler turned out on demand. Odets told Michael J. Mendelsohn that he had always held the play "a little in contempt for that reason," although he came to think it better than he had at first imagined. It is difficult, however, to take *Golden Boy* as a false jewel in the artist's crown. It is too close to the other Odets plays in tone, in style, in social point. If the original impulse to write it was more practical than pure, the subject matter was close to the author's heart. "So many artists today stand in relation to Hollywood as our hero in relation to his double career," Clurman wrote in his introduction to *Golden Boy,* which he called Odets's "most subjective play." Even before Odets went to Hollywood and before he received the less lucrative applause of Broadway, he worried about the nature of American success in *Awake and Sing!* Add self-doubt to preexisting social concern and Odets brought more to *Golden Boy* than a desire to rescue the Group. It was a problem he would return to again, more directly if less effectively, in *The Big Knife.*

Although Odets had written Joe Bonaparte for John (then Jules) Garfield, the role went to Luther Adler. Clurman gave good professional reasons for that choice in *The Fervent Years,* but one suspects an echo from the past. Adler had been Sol Ginsberg in John Howard Lawson's *Success Story,* and although the two plays are not much alike, the theme is the same (distintegration brought on by success) and there is a certain gruff likeness between Joe and Sol, especially as we meet them in the opening scenes of the two plays.

Golden Boy turned out to be a success story in fact. The play, directed by Clurman, opened at the Belasco Theatre on November 4, 1937. The reviews were mixed, some regretting Odets's fall from serious drama, some simply enthusiastic, almost none paying attention to the play's social point; yet, they were "business notices," as Clurman said in *The Fervent Years,* the kind of reviews that, even while dispraising, make audiences want to come to the theater. The play ran for 250 performances; there was a West Coast production, directed by Stella Adler; the Group took the play on the road and, then, sent a non-Group company to cities it had not reached; there was a London engagement after the New York closing and a Paris production in late 1938. In was the first Odets play to sell to the movies (and the last until the 1950s); the film, released September 1939, stayed close to the Odets original, except for a happy ending, and used at least one group member, Lee J. Cobb, who repeated the part of Mr. Bonaparte which he had played in the West Coast production. "By money standards, *Golden Boy* was the greatest success in the Group's history," wrote Clurman; it made enough "to sustain the Group for two seasons." The play was revived for a limited engagement on March 12, 1952 with Garfield as Joe and Odets as his own director; the reviews were generally more respectful than they had been in 1937. At the time of his death, Odets was working on a musical version of *Golden Boy* and when it materialized in 1964, he was listed as co-author with William Gibson; although his plot is there and the social implications (transposed to the black-white situation), there is nothing of Odets in the language.

Burns Mantle, who liked *Golden Boy,* guessed that the smart money would brand it "typical picture stuff, save for the unhappy ending," and a number of critics did point to the boxing milieu as a Hollywood cliché. Charles E. Dexter in the *Daily Worker* was the most specific, pointing to *Kid Galahad,* which had been released in May of that year, and finding that Lorna "is really none other than the good-hearted, sensitive but throughly hard-boiled good bad-woman popularized by Miss Bette Davis of Hollywood." That film had not only the "good bad-woman," the manager's girl in an incipient romance with the boxer, but gangsters and comic hangers-on as well. The criticism was accurate without necessarily being just. The influence of the movies is clear even in the word "fadeout" at the end of scenes. Odets defended himself in an article in the New York *Times* in which he called the movies "the folk theatre of America," said that Hollywood "has great talent for picking important American types and interesting and vital themes" and wondered why the serious playwright could not use for his own purposes what is only exploited in films. "This was attempted in 'Golden Boy.'" There is something slightly after-the-fact in Odets's statement; I suspect that it is a fair description of what he did rather than what he consciously set out to do. In a serious statement in *Figaro,* a positive reprise of negative American criticism, Henriette Pascar, who presented *Golden Boy* in Paris, commented on the valuable influence Hollywood had been on Odets. Joe Bonaparte, then, is the brother to all those other young men, in plays and films, who come innocent into the fight game, smash their way to the top and, usually, taste the ashes in success. There is nothing in that kinship that need demean Joe as a character or cheapen the theme of the play.

Joe's motive for becoming a boxer is a double one. He presumably wants the material rewards of success although that is clear only in his desire for a car and in the lines of other characters (Lorna's "You want your arm in *gelt* up to the elbow"). He also wants revenge for past insults ("People have hurt my feelings for years")—the cock-eye and the funny name—and protection against future pain. This is shown dramatically in his violent reaction to Moody's jokes at his expense in I, 1 and his chip-on-the-shoulder entrance in I, 2 ("I don't want to be criticized!") in which he expects an attack that does not come. Joe's vulnerability and his pugnaciousness, established in those scenes, continue throughout the play as we see him with Lorna, with Moody, with the reporters, even with Eddie and Tokio. "I don't like myself, past, present and future," says Joe in I, 2, in a speech that ends, "Tomorrow's my birthday! I change my life!" For that birthday, Mr. Bonaparte has bought Joe an expensive violin, and that gift, as symbol and as prop, is the alternative the play offers Joe. The choice, as Moody recognizes in I, 3, is between "the fist" and "the fiddle."

Some critics (see Eleanor Flexner's *American Playwrights: 1918–1938*), reacting realistically to a non-realistic device, worried about the appropriateness of the violinist's hands in boxing gloves. The problem with the symbol lies elsewhere, in the likelihood that the audience may respond positively to Carp's doubts (he says the violin "looks like a coffin for a baby"), may see Joe as an image of the artist in an uncongenial world. If music is to be taken as a bona fide alternative for Joe, Carp's question, "could a boy make a living playing this instrument in our competitive civilization today?" must be rejected as beside the point—as it is by Mr. Bonaparte when he says, "He don't need it, to be millionaire. A good life'sa possible—" Odets may assume that there is something intrinsically good in music or in Frank's life as a CIO organizer, but these things are good in the context of the play because they are right for the characters. "Whatever you got ina your nature to do isa not foolish!" says the old man to Carp and later, to Joe: "You no gotta nature for fight." Frank brings the music metaphor full circle in the last scene, "The pleasure of acting as you think! The satisfaction of staying where you belong, being what you are . . . at harmony with millions of others!" Joe senses this, as his speech on the comforts of music in I, 4 indicates, but he cannot reject Carp's "competitive civilization" and so dismisses the violin as an insufficient weapon: "If music shot bullets I'd like it better—" One of the weaknesses in the play is that Joe's self-pity sometimes drowns the social character in too obvious psychology (unhappy childhood) and, thus, endangers both the dramatic and the thematic pattern of the play.

By the end of Act I, Joe has chosen fist over fiddle; he tells Lorna this in I, 4 and acts it out in the next scene in which, after trying the birthday violin (a farewell performance, off stage), he gives it back to his father. Mr. Bonaparte refuses to bless that decision: "But I don't gonna give no word!" Act II makes it impossible for Joe to retreat to his earlier position. The irrevocability lies not so much in the breaking of his hand at the end of the act as in the change in him of which the broken hand is only a "fadeout" image. He has already let Eddie Fuseli "buy a piece" of him (II, 1) and his behavior before he goes into the ring, his "Eddie's the only one here who understands me" followed by Eddie's pep talk, punctuated with destruction words ("kill Lombardo!" "Tear his skull off!"), convinces his father that he is lost: "I give-a you every word to fight . . . I sorry for you."

Although Siggie, Joe's brother-in-law, has lines like "My god is success" and Carp's pessimism often seems to uphold the ethic of the boxing world, the family scenes (unfortunately much less vivid than those in *Awake and Sing!*) are designed as dramatic instances of the good life. The play states this much more effectively in a negative way, in the disconnection among the characters in the boxing world, in the Moody-Lorna scenes, in Eddie's menacing motherliness, even in Roxy's comic bumptiousness. In conventional revolt against the first, Joe goes into the second and finds no comfort in his success there. The title contender is as lonely, as much "on an island" (I, 4) as the young man who first enters Moody's office. Joe turns to Lorna: "You're real for me—the way music was real." Lorna and music become one in the touching "whistling duet" (II, 2), but if we do not react too sentimentally to that scene we may remember later that they never whistle together, that each picks up the other's last note and carries on alone. There is no salvation for Joe in Lorna for she is tied to the system both by plot and theme. Like Judy in *The General Died at Dawn*, she sets out to manipulate the hero and ends by falling in love with him. *Golden Boy* is no "adventure-romance," however; there can be no blissful "fadeout" because Joe comes to Lorna not for love, but for a substitute for his violated nature. In a discussion of Group acting in *New Theatres for Old*, Mordecai Gorelik explained that Frances Farmer, who played Lorna, was given the action of "helping others" as the basis of her role. Such a "spine" might help the actress react to any other performer within a scene, but the total impact of the character depends on our recognizing that her instinct to be helpful is in fact a withdrawal; she vacillates between Moody and Joe, going where the "need" is strongest (how the word "need" echoes through her scenes), because giving comfort is less risky than giving love. "All I want is peace and quiet, not love," she says, confirming what Joe has just said, "And now you're dead." Metaphor emphasizes the absence of life: Joe, a commodity, sold in pieces like yard goods, complains of Moody, "He treats me like a possession!" but a few lines later, he laments to Lorna, "Why don't you belong to me . . ."

A number of critics—for instance, Richard Lockridge and Gilbert Seldes—questioned the inevitability of the play's fatal ending. I could understand objecting to the ludicrous overpreparation for the death by automobile: the boxer killed in "a big, red Stutz" in I, 1; Siggie's line about Joe's driving in I, 2; the play of the traffic lights and Joe's speed speeches in I, 4; the worry over Joe's Duesenberg in Act II. I could accept that Lorna's "We'll find some city . . ." speech, so like the usual Odets lyric optimism, might mislead an audience not willing to see that she is responding to "need," not hope. But I cannot understand going outside the play for other possibilities (as Seldes did in giving it a biographical reading) or writing off the "accident" as an "easy solution" (Lockridge's phrase) when it is not a solution at all, but a confirmation of what has already happened in the play. The alternatives have been wiped out for Joe by II, 4, when his father gives up on him. We see this visually in III, 1, when he dresses like Eddie, and hear it in Lorna's words, "You murdered that boy with the generous face—God knows where you hid the body!" Joe says the same thing after he kills the Chocolate Drop in the ring, "I murdered myself, too!" Joe and Lorna can no more get away than Moody can "take my girl and we go sit by the river and it's everything." Their deaths are only a last illustration of the quality of their lives as the play has defined them. Since speed is an escape for Joe, one that he describes in terms of aggression, violence, separateness, the automobile is a fitting means of execution. Nor is there any point in quibbling over whether or not the crash is suicide; the important thing to recognize is that, even if it is an accident, it is no accident.

Golden Boy, then, is another Faustian variation, the story of a young man who sells his soul (goes against his nature) and discovers, too late, that he has made a bad bargain. As such, it is obviously attractive to audiences, and it has the added virtues of a character like Moody (the sad dregs of Joe's boyish dreams) and of dialogue, particularly in the boxing-world scenes, which, in the best Odets fashion, is amusing even while it works into the play's theme. There is one last step that the play expects the audience to take and they do not always go along—as the original reviews indicate. Odets intends an analogy between boxing and capitalism. This is clear not simply from the presence of Eddie Fuseli, the businessman-gangster, but in a consistent pattern of lines. "It's a business," says Moody and goes on to compare Joe to the telephone. He is regularly an instrument, a machine or a commodity, a possession. They discuss his marketability (hitting is good business). This is emphasized in the final scene in which the two worlds meet, the one to mourn the loss of a property, the other the loss of a man. The words *kill* and *murder,* conventional enough in the boxing context, have a condemnatory use in the play, building to Frank's *"You're all killers!"* It was not simply that Joe went against his nature, but that he never recognized that music was his way of fighting against a "life . . . printed on dollar bills."

XI. *"When I'm happy I'm a different person"*

Aᴄᴄᴏʀᴅɪɴɢ ᴛᴏ a note in the New York *Daily News* (January 31, 1938), *The Silent Partner* was being postponed until the next season, but when that season came *Rocket to the Moon* was the Clifford Odets play the Group Theatre presented. The playwright, writing in the New York *World-Telegram* after the opening of *Rocket,* said, "The roots of love and the meaning of it in the present world need surely to be comprehended as much as the effect of a strike on its activists." His remark was partly defensive, a response to the reviews, but it was also an accurate indication of a new emphasis in his work. "Mr. Odets seems to have discovered the subject in the course of quarreling and reconciling with his wife, Luise Rainer," Ira Wolfert wrote in his NANA review. However accurate Wolfert's gossipy assumption, Odets did move at this time of marital troubles into the first of three plays in which social problems were subsumed in emotional ones and the triangle *(Rocket, Clash by Night)* or the boy-meets-girl story *(Night Music)* became the central plot.

When *Rocket* went into rehearsal in Boston (where the Group was doing *Golden Boy*) in October 1938, the play was still in the making. Harold Clurman, who, as usual, directed, reported in *The Fervent Years* that the last act was not completed until ten days before the opening, November 24, 1938. The play got a mixed reception. Some reviewers welcomed it simply as a "romance" (Odets's own descriptive subtitle); others thought, sadly, that it lacked substance. Arthur Pollock, who admired the play, suggested that Odets must have followed the advice of those critics who wanted a non-propaganda play only to find that they really wanted plays that said something. The most persistent criticisms were that the play was confused, the last act too long and the protagonist's awakening unacceptable. Early in December an attempt was made to correct some of the presumed deficiencies. "He has not cut in chunks but has whittled," Richard Lockridge reported in a second review, praising the new version. It was not all trimming, however. One character, the tire salesman in Act III, was taken out completely (he was back in for the London production in 1948), and the ending was altered through rewriting as well as cutting. There is no indication that the surgery increased the life of the play. It ran for 131 performances. On March 7, 1939, *Awake and Sing!* went into repertory with the new play, but by then the *Rocket* had pretty much run its course.

The Playviewer in the Bronx *Home News* dismissed *Rocket,* accusing Odets of again using "a conventional Hollywood plot, this time that of the 'office wife.'" If one stays at the level of surface event in the play, the analogy is a shrewd one, for in the conventional office-wife movie of the 1930s, the husband, moved by proximity and a desire for change, turns to the secretary (usually stopping short of adultery, however) but comes back to the wife. This is the ostensible plot of *Rocket to the Moon*. The first act establishes the characters and the mood (the economic and spiritual depression from which all of them want to escape) and plants the possibility—for the characters as well as the audience—of an affair between Ben Stark, the drab dentist, and Cleo Singer, his naively knowing office girl. Act II initiates the affair. There is a structural weakness in this act in that Odets puts his characters and the audience through the same emotional development twice. In both scenes, Ben moves through a conflict of desire and guilt to a kiss at the curtain. An audience, conditioned by the conventions of the stage, is likely to assume that the embrace at the end of II, 1 is an indication that the affair has begun; such an assumption makes a good part of II, 2 unintelligible until we realize that, despite the intimacy of the nose-pulling scene, the couple has not advanced beyond the kiss. There is a reason for the two scenes. In II, 1, it is Cleo who declares her love; in II, 2, Ben, largely in reaction to his wife's suspicions, moves from passive to active, and becomes, for the moment, at least, the dominant male that Belle will not let him be. Although such a development is necessary for the character, the repetitive pattern of the two scenes is disconcerting. In the last act, realizing that his and Cleo's love cannot continue, Ben returns to Belle. A standard triangle play, then, but Odets is interested in something more than the skeleton story on which he hangs his play. He is concerned with the social and psychological situation which gives rise to the affair and its effect on the two main characters.

In a jaw-breaking sentence in the *World-Telegram* article, Odets insisted that *Rocket* "attempts to depict the difficulty or near-impossibility of full and natural love between man and woman in a society where each one of us is reduced to a high tension of loneliness by the competitive set-up and the passion for personal triumph." Or, as Phil Cooper puts it in the play, "Who's got time to think about women! I'm trying to make a living!" In *Rocket*, as in the earlier plays, Odets has brought together a number of disparate types each of whom represents the dislocation in the world by the way he copes or fails to cope with it. That dislocation, as in *Awake and Sing!* and *Paradise Lost*, is economic (*Rocket* is another Depression play, fittingly enough after the recession of 1937–38), but it is much more than that; it is a spiritual state in which no one dares risk anything. "Why don't you suddenly ride away, an airplane, a boat!" Mr. Prince says to Ben. "Take a rocket to the moon! Explode!" If Ben and Cleo do explode to the extent of an affair—and within the context of the play that is a positive act which leads to positive consequences—most of the characters have been defused by events (Cooper) or have defused themselves (Frenchy, Willy Wax). It is through Cooper that Odets makes overt social criticism: "Why can't I make a living? I'm falling apart by inches. . . . Where will it end if they can't use millions of Coopers?" Frenchy, the foot doctor, has settled for the "small change" of life and worries that Cleo will unsettle Ben who has done the same: "He spends his days trying to exhaust himself so he can fall asleep quick." Willy Wax has Hollywood success but has become, in his own words, "a mechanical man in a mechanical era!" Until she finds the courage to act, Cleo vacillates between the reality which cows her, as any of the characters can by speaking sharply, and a fantasy life in which an imaginary career (modeling, dancing) and an imaginary family ("My parents wanted to send me to a fashionable girl's college") rescue her from the ugliness of her life. Even Mr. Prince, obviously the most vital character in the play, has a joking manner which is his protection; financially successful, he remains a lonely man wanting to move in with the daugher who hates him, willing to marry a Cleo who does not love him. When he finally risks being the clown his daughter thinks he is, exposes himself in the last act, it is too late; Cleo rejects him. "Next week I'll buy myself a dog. . . ."

The marriage of Ben and Belle is presented as a product of the society they live in. Ben sees them as "two machines counting up the petty cash," and Prince says, "She runs his life like a credit manager." The implication is that for the Starks, as for the Bergers, the family is an economic unit and that social fact has made a tyrant of Belle, a younger, more frightened and more waspish Bessie. Abortively fruitful (the child that died at birth), this marriage—like that of Sam Katz in *Lost*—is a childless one, but, as the talk of adoption indicates, it is used here less as a sterility image than as an indication that Belle's potentialities, like those of Cooper, are not being properly employed. Belle or the marriage has emasculated Ben, turned him into a baby (Belle: "Any day now I'm expecting to have to powder and diaper you"), an obedient pet (Cleo: "He stands there like a big shepherd dog and she tells him what to do!"), an iceberg (Prince: "three-quarters under water"). This is illustrated dramatically in the first act in which he caves in under her insistence that they not risk a new, more expensive office and in his mannerisms (his nervous smile) by which he apologizes for his kindliness, a dangerous quality in Belle's practical world. Since Belle is more than simple economic woman, her opposition to the new office stems partly from the fact that it is Mr. Prince, her father, who has offered to finance it and she cannot forgive him for his treatment of her mother, to whom he did not speak for ten years. That marriage, if we can believe the survivor, was also an economic operation ("with their bills they ate holes in me") which demeaned the provider ("she insulted my soul"). Prince's description ("Play safe! A housewife's conception of life!") makes it sound like the Stark marriage and in fact, Belle, trying to escape her mother's fate, has recreated her parents' marriage in her own.

Only a confirmed environmentalist would lay the blame for the spiritual and emotional displacement of all the characters on the socioeconomic doorstep of the system. Odets is such a diagnostician in the *World-Telegram* article quoted above. Although, as a creator of character, he can suggest psychological subtleties, his play is finally based on the assumption that society created the characters. Although Frenchy has settled for less himself, he is a character through whom Odets seems to speak (the stage directions make much of him as observer) and his long speeches in Act III dismiss love as a solution to life's problems.

> Love is a beginning, a jumping-off place. . . . Who's got time and place for 'love and the grace to use it'? . . . You have to bring a whole balanced normal life to love if you want it to go! . . . I don't see much normal life. . . . the free exercise of love, I figure, gets harder every day.

Implicit in this description is the suggestion that love (happiness, the full life) would become possible only if the environment were altered. Change the circumstances and you change the psychology, or, as Cooper puts it, "When I'm happy I'm a different person." Although with *Rocket* Odets has moved a distance from the early plays, this description of the play's social bedrock indicates that the situation cries out for another Ralph, another Leo to point toward the promised land.

The pointer is Cleo and the promise is a great deal more amorphous than it was in *Awake* or *Lost*. She rejects Wax ("his type loves himself"), Prince ("you're too old for me") and—after watching him fail to recreate himself for her sake—Ben ("He's a citizen of another country"). "None of you can give me what I'm looking for: a whole full world, with all the trimmings!" She

sets out in search of a place where love is possible. It is unfortu-
nate, I think, that the word *need* turns up in her key line, "I
want a love that uses me, that needs me," for *need* has been
used in contrast to *love* elsewhere in the play (as in *Golden
Boy*), but *use* is correctly there since the proper use of human
beings is one of the play's major themes. According to Clurman,
Luise Rainer said that Cleo should have married Mr. Prince.
The suggestion makes good sense in the practical world
(European realism vs. American romanticism), but Odets wants
at least one of his characters to escape the make-do world in
which they are trapped. One of the problems with the play is
that the vessel for his romantic aspiration is a weak one. Cleo
may be "true," as Clurman said, but she is "uneducated, child-
ish, rattle-brained" as well, as he also said, and there is no one
in the play (Frenchy is an unpleasant mystery to her) to help
lead her to the position from which she can see into the future.
Her one positive quality is that she is willing to take risks—to
declare her love for Ben, to go to Wax's office, to date
Prince—but Odets's depiction of her as naive and a little foolish
makes these decisions seem almost accidental, elicited by whatever is said around her. Odets took a risk of his own when he let
Prince respond to her stated quest with, "You'll go down the
road alone—like Charlie Chaplin?" for the image is a good one
and it embodies not real hope but the sentimental longing for
the happy land.

Even if we accept that foolish little Cleo—like self-pitying
Ralph and confused Leo—can suddenly see beyond the horizon,
there is a problem in the play's ending. Odets wants to suggest
that for Ben, too, the affair has been a positive, a replenishing
experience. In the earlier version of the play, this point was
made more forcefully. The salesman who appears abruptly in
Act III brings the possibility of a happy marriage even in terrible times. Frenchy seems to dismiss him ("He asks for little and
gets little"), but his description comes in a speech in which he
separates the ordinary from the special and puts Ben in the second category. This implies that what the salesman does in small
Ben can do more grandly. Then, there is a second awakening to
strengthen Ben. A purposeful Cooper comes in search of a den-
tal magazine (although it is difficult to see how reading an arti-

cle will bring in non-existent patients) and he and Ben leave together for the beach, for Belle, for the future. That version of the play ends on the word "Awake . . ." (an echo that distressed a number of reviewers), an allusion to the metaphor that still exists in the present play in Ben's "A man falls asleep in marriage." Perhaps because actions that were intended to reinforce Ben's decision actually distracted audiences from it, the reviewers tended to disbelieve the final positive statement.

The ending is cleaner but even more difficult to accept in the revised version. "I insist this is a beginning. Do you hear?—I insist," Ben cries and doubt starts in the listener's mind: the dentist doth protest too much, methinks. There are two difficulties—one dramatic, one thematic—which stand in the way of Ben's insistence. His resolute action, the initiation of the affair, in II, 2 is lost in his behavior in the last act; convinced by Frenchy and Prince that he can offer Cleo only a version of his marriage to Belle, he gives her up, but his method of doing so (the broken, stumbling speeches, the oblique anger at Prince, the refusal to speak directly to Cleo) makes even that gesture irresolute. Thematically, since he represents one of the middle-class possibilities Cleo rejects, a positive reading of the character would seem to be ruled out by the philosophy behind the play. At the end, the lights of the Hotel Algiers, which has been a symbol of adventure in the play, can be seen in the dark office. This visual effect is to suggest the light of possibility in Ben's dark world, I assume, but, like the muted ending, it has as much regret as resolution in it. Oddly, it is that air of regret that is most pervasive and most attractive in *Rocket to the Moon*.

XII. *"I am in love with the possibilities, the human possibilities"*

BURNS MANTLE, in his review of *Night Music*, suggested that the play resulted when Clifford Odets, like Mr. Prince in *Rocket to the Moon*, began to wonder what went on in the Hotel Algiers. Up close, where we can see the "Riffraff," as Ben calls the inhabitants of the Algiers, the hotel is no longer a call to life; it is another image of American society. Perhaps less consciously than the hotel name, two other elements from *Rocket* went into *Night Music*. In the earlier version of *Rocket*, Cleo says, "Yes, like in a story—'Once upon a time'—But I'd like that here, right on earth." In the finished play, Cooper says, "Who rests in the front-line trench? I suddenly realized life is a war . . ." *Night Music* is Cleo's fairy tale played against Cooper's war.

On August 23, 1939, the New York *Times* announced that *The Silent Partner* was being shelved once again and that Odets was about to "begin work on 'Night Music,' a play with incidental music to be ready for rehearsal by December." It was. There was a deal of publicity that month on the search for the feminine lead (apparently no theatrical organization, however dedicated, could quite escape the Scarlett O'Hara virus), and Alvah Bessie, while wrongly predicting success for the play, lamented that Group regulars had been passed over for a movie star (Jane Wyatt). More than the heroine came from Hollywood. Two independent film makers, Albert Lewin and David H.

Loew, helped finance the production in exchange for movie rights and Odets's services on the script. Joseph T. Shipley saw Odetsian corruption in what I take as an inside joke—Steve's use of Al Lewin's name in the play. *Night Music* opened in Boston on February 8, 1940—the first Odets play to have an out-of-town tryout—to mixed notices, friendly, sad reviews that compared the play to William Saroyan's *The Time of Your Life* and Elmer Rice's *Two on an Island*, both then playing in New York. The same, generally negative reviews followed the New York opening at the Broadhurst (February 22), and the play closed after twenty performances. In *The Fervent Years,* Harold Clurman gave an account of the second-guessing that followed the unhappy opening, the search for something (the theater, the sets, the director) to blame, an accusatory period in which he decided not to direct the next Odets play. He never directed another. In June, Odets went to Hollywood to work on the screenplay of *Music;* by January 1941, the film had been canceled. In February 1951, *Night Music,* somewhat revised, was staged by the Equity Library Theatre; Fay was played by Bette Grayson, who had had a walk-on in 1940, married Odets in 1943 and would divorce him before 1951 was out. The production was moved to the ANTA Playhouse on April 8, 1951 (at about the same time there was a revival at the Jefferson Theater Workshop); the reviews of the ANTA revival were more harsh than the original ones had been and it closed after eight performances. Clurman, this time an outsider looking on, restated his admiration for the play and suggested that it failed because "the audience refuses to identify his homeless world as theirs." I confess, never having seen it, that *Night Music* is one of the Odets plays for which I have the greatest affection.

The comparison between *Night Music* and *Two on an Island* is negligible, resulting presumably from the fact that Rice, like Odets, has a young couple, a gallery of types and Manhattan as backdrop. Saroyan is a more interesting case. In the New York *Times* piece that became the introduction to the published play, Clurman took umbrage at the comparison, assuming—as Brooks Atkinson had ("Now that Odets writes like Saroyan, Doomsday is near")—that there was something nefarious in it. In fact, the mood of the two works is very similar: a painful playfulness through which the dramatist moves haltingly toward a positive statement. In *The Fervent Years*, Clurman himself described *The Time of Your Life* in terms of "lyric anarchism and confused benevolence" which he called "the characteristic tone of the early forties," but it is difficult to see how the "gentle and melancholy" tone of *Night Music* is that different.

The texture of *Night Music,* as Clurman indicated in his introduction, grows out of the fact that Odets's characters "are fundamentally *homeless,* and, whether or not they know it, they are in search of a home, of something real, secure, dependable in a slippery, shadowy, noisy and nervous world." The description is an accurate one so long as we recognize that *secure* and *dependable* are used in a special way, to exclude the material security that Eddie Bellows ("graceless and funny") wants to offer Fay. Although the play is full of characters who would probably settle for less, *home* here (like the world Cleo is seeking in *Rocket)* is a place where lives need not be, as Fay says her parents' are, "narrow, petty and small!" In his list of the characters and how they reflect the homelessness in the play (Mrs. Scott's dressing room curtains, the man in the phone booth trying to make connections), Clurman passed too quickly over the sailor. It is true that he is after his "bit of fun," but as the scene is designed, he turns from desk clerk to bellboy to whore, insisting "but you know me," asking, as Steve does all through the play, to be recognized. The homeless theme is emphasized, as Winifred L. Dusenbury has pointed out, by the effective use of suitcase as prop (it is lost, found, moved around, passed from one person to another) and by the fact that ten of the twelve scenes end with the exit of characters for another destination. The theme can even be heard in Al's improvised pop song about "a penthouse built for two."

One way of getting the quality described above would be an accumulation of realistic detail, but that was never the intention of *Night Music*. Rosamond Gilder, commenting on the direction, said, ". . . realism is there but it is wedded to a pictorial stylization." Most of the characters in the play are simple cartoons, affectionate or satiric sketches carried by a single quirk, and they arrive and leave with minimal preparation. One reason for

139

this is that the whole play is a fairy tale on the Hollywood model (the off-stage nonsense with the monkeys that initiates the action cries out for the screen)—a boy-meets-girl story in which the slow coming together is overseen (and blessed) by an avuncular, elderly man (Detective A. L. Rosenberger), a fairy godfather with almost supernatural powers. A *deus*, Joseph Wood Krutch called him, and he does enter—returning Steve's stolen suitcase in I, 2—on the young man's sneering repetition of his own earlier line, "God is where He was before!" Rosenberger's omnipresence and his talent for recovering lost suitcases might be explained naturally (a good detective, after all), but his powers come, in fact, from his function as device. There is a certain theatrical outrageousness in the blatant way Odets uses him, not simply in his comings and goings, but in his sententiousness ("I am in love with the possibilities, the human possibilities") and in the fatal disease (the cancer that killed Steve's mother) that Odets gives him. The disease has a thematic use in the play (that a dying man—in contrast to the dead-in-life like Fay's father—may espouse life); but I am convinced that Odets chose so risky a contrivance (how Atkinson complained of it in his *Times* column for March 3) mainly to set up the scene in II, 5 in which Steve's big mouth traps him into an outrage ("I'll live to see you on a slab!") which is more appalling to him than to Rosenberger. The scene is pure schmaltz (as are several others: the couple's sleeping on the park bench, the clarinet ending their quarrel) and intentionally so; it is a stage in the education of Steve, but it is also meant to produce a lump in the audience throat.

"What's he think we are, that Dick?" snarls Steve at one point and adds, emphasizing the artificiality of the play, "Orphans of the storm?" So they are, at least until they learn the predictable Odets lesson and cease to be victims. Both of Steve's parents are dead, his father killed in the First World War, and his solitary struggle for existence is played against the background of economic need: "They slammed me outa twenty states—I was up for vagrancy in five!" (Historical note: unemployment figures were higher in 1939 than in 1935.) Steve's response to his situation is a multiple one: he retreats into the safe past ("There's like a smell of geraniums an' I hear my mother say . . .") or, like Cleo, concocts a fantasy life ("I'm a big man in Hollywood"). But his chief defense is anger, a constant flow of verbal abuse and threats ("I test with the fists"). He is remarkably ineffective in his tough-guy pose since he is roughed up by the stagehand (I, 2) and the bellboy (I, 4) and, when he successfully rises to Fay's defense (II, 1), the man he thinks is eyeing her turns out to be blind. Alvah Bessie saw Steve as "the young Odets, the young American"; less biographical and less general, John Anderson, who disliked the play, recognized the hero as "the sensitive, rebellious young man . . . blood brother" to Ralph in *Awake and Sing!* and Joe in *Golden Boy.* The lineage is correct, but Steve has a busier mouth than either of the early angry young men had. He is sometimes funny and sometimes gradiose, in the tall-tale tradition ("I'm an eighty octane guy—Ethyl in my veins—and I'm sore as hell!"), but frequently just offensive—or would be if the lines were removed from the context of his personality. "And yet, with all his noise, he makes a good impression," says Rosenberger, but many critics disagreed, echoing the judgment of Helen Eager in the Boston *Traveller:* "He is probably the most unsympathetic, egotistical, insufferable liar that has been foisted on the public in many moons." I'm with Rosenberger.

If Steve is a somewhat unusual hero, Fay is conventional enough. Her blandness may be a necessary contrast to his flamboyance, but it occasionally endangers her scenes, making her almost disappear. She does have spunk (she stands up to her father, to Eddie, even to Steve), but *spunk* is a polite kind of determination. She is not poor ("Almost," she says and Odets describes her as "lower-middle-class"), not fighting Steve's battle. What she wants to escape, as her long, circumstantial speech in I, 5 indicates, is a Philadelphia in which "Nothing, nothing, I tell you nothing happens!" Eddie, once her fiance, misunderstands her longing, praises it ("she *should* want more") as evidence of American material drive. Steve insists that his "whole manner's anticupid" and Rosenberger says "not one human thought came out of your mouth." She wants Steve because "he understands that life is no half-way business."

It is not enough that Rosenberger help rout the forces from Philly and bring the lovers together. The conventional ending of this kind of story will not do for Odets. No one can escape on the wings of doves (Fay reads Psalm 55:1-6 in II, 5) or of angels (Roy whistles "The Prisoner's Song" in I, 5). It is false courage to take comfort in the "Night music" of crickets (Fay: "If they can sing, I can sing") because, as a furious Steve says, "What kinda life where you gotta compare yourself to crickets? *They're bugs!*" Steve has to learn to make his anger less indiscriminate (Rosenberger: "your anger must bear children or it's hopeless"), which he does by accepting himself, putting aside the Hollywood dreams and going for a world in which he and Fay can be used to the full ("I propose a shoe to fit my foot, not bigger"). The bulk of the ideational statement in the play comes in II, 4, at the World's Fair, where the theme of the fair (the world of tomorrow) can be used effectively and where the feet of the gigantic George Washington statue (like A. L. Rosenberger's name: Abraham Lincoln) can insist that Steve's is a very American quest. *"Make this America for us!"* At the end of the play, in telling Steve that he must make it himself, Rosenberger pulls the audience back to the historical allusion: " 'The preservation of the sacred fire of liberty . . . is in the hands of the people.' Washington said that—it's on the statue."

This fairly direct statement is complicated by the way in which Odets uses the war. Roy, the young man Steve meets in the park, is going to "join the war," and Steve decides that if he loses his messenger boy's job over the monkey mix-up he will do the same. Roy, who turns up again in the World's Fair scene, is, for Odets, *a specter, an image of* Steve's *war thoughts.* For Steve, the army is a last resort in a world in which "I vamp around an' I vamp around an' nothing happens—you can't get a start." We are back again with Sid's "dumb basketball player" in *Waiting for Lefty*, but the war is not, as it was then, a vaguely projected imperialist war. World War II is on in Europe, as the play itself indicates through the man in I, 3 worried about his relatives in Poland. When Rosenberg enlists Steve in Cooper's war ("your fight is here, not across the water"), one cannot help remembering that *Night Music* turned up between August 1939 (the Nazi-Soviet pact) and June 1941 (the invasion of Russia) and its pacifism is suspect. Played today, out of its immediate political context, it might work more easily with a growing pacifist mood that distrusts the American presence abroad.

The published play gives no evidence at all (except for a note in which Odets thanks Hanns Eisler) and the reviews are somewhat confused on the subject, but the general impression I have is that *Night Music* was unusual in its attempt to present a total theater experience in which text, performance, music and sets worked together to convey a prevailing mood. The Group had always worked for an effective ensemble, a total impression, and Mordecai Gorelik had been insisting that sets must contribute to a play's dramatic and ideational impulse, but in *Night Music,* design and music reached out as bridges between scenes. While the many scene shifts were being made, slides were projected on the front curtain, "calligraphic in their design," Gorelik told me, in which musical notes formed the furniture; as Rosamond Gilder described them, they were "amusing, ornamental devices" which had a useful function, each pointing to the locale of the scene to come. Paul Bowles, himself a Group composer *(My Heart's in the Highlands)*, praised Eisler's score, but complained that "ninety-five percent" of the music was "used for scene shifting." What seems clear is that the Gorelik slides and the Eisler score were supposed to sustain the mood of the play which might have been broken by time lapses. The music, Bowles said, was completely rewritten while the play was in rehearsal so that new sequences replaced those that had come "to seem insufficient or incongruous." Gorelik's sets, he wrote me, were "vignettes on small platforms" with painted backdrops that looked like neon lights, close in tone to "Eisler's score, which was dry and modern, but melodic." Odets told an interviewer that "I don't see it [New York] visually—though it's beautiful enough—so much as I hear it and feel it." I suspect that Eisler's music (which is not available) and even Gorelik's sets were designed to heighten the sound and feel of the city in *Night Music.*

XIII. *"No manhood in the boy!"*

He wanted the devotion of the man in the cellar and the congratulations of the boys at '21.' He wanted the praise of the philosophers and the votes of *Variety*'s box-score." *He* is Clifford Odets, of course, and the lines are Harold Clurman's, his recollection—not exactly in tranquility—of the quarrels that followed the opening of *Night Music.* Earlier in *The Fervent Years,* Clurman had described a "first skirmish," a session in London in 1938 in which Odets complained, "I'm tired of the Group company." It seems clear that Odets wanted out as much as he wanted in, that he could not break with the Group (his family, his home), but that he was as restless there as Ralph in the Berger apartment, itching for the kind of flamboyant success that was so often his subject. With *Clash by Night,* he got Broadway at its noisiest and thereby hangs a tale.

While the play was still running, Odets published excerpts from a journal in which one can see the slow growth of what was then called "The Trio Play." The idea emerged in May 1940; writing began over the summer; the political theme became clear by October although Vince, its embodiment, was not invented until November. A second draft of the play was finished by December 4. A simple story of the artist at work: the making of a play. The next step: the breaking of a play. Odets had originally planned to produce the play himself, out of the

144

Group Theatre office, with Luther Adler and Sylvia Sidney in the leads. Unable to find backing, Odets turned to his Sutton Place neighbor, Billy Rose, and the Group was out. The play, originally scheduled for spring production in 1941, was postponed for want of a juvenile. "Tell that one to the thousand odd youthful members of Equity who are now idle and hear them laugh," wrote Burns Mantle. When the play went into production in the fall, Tallulah Bankhead had the starring role; Lee Strasberg (as director), Lee J. Cobb (as Jerry) and Art Smith (in a bit as a drunk) were the only Group veterans in evidence. By that time, the Group itself was dead.

The play opened in Detroit on October 27, 1941, and then moved on to Baltimore. The reviewers in both cities were friendly—with reservations; it was generally agreed that the play could stand some changes. Pittsburgh was the third stop on the pre-Broadway tour, and it was there that the trouble began. According to Polly Rose Gottlieb, whose foolish, anecdotal book about her brother, *The Nine Lives of Billy Rose*, may not be exactly a disinterested source, Bankhead at that point refused to read a new scene Odets had written. Whatever triggered the ill-feeling, the battle, it quickly became clear, was between the star and the producer. Both Mrs. Gottlieb and Miss Bankhead (in her autobiography *Tallulah*) agree that billing was the basis of contention, a proposed sign "Billy Rose Presents Tallulah Bankhead . . ." which made the actress furious. The production trailed its rancorous way from Pittsburgh to Philadelphia, shooting off sparks that warmed the hearts of gossip columnists everywhere. In Philadelphia, after playing the opening night with a 103° temperature (105°, said Miss Bankhead), suffering from what the Philadelphia *Public Ledger* called "a severe case of influenza" ("double pneumonia," said Miss Bankhead), the star was whisked to a hospital, and the last pre-Broadway run was canceled. That there were other tensions is clear from the account by Joseph Schildkraut (who played Earl) in *My Father and I:* "But between Miss Bankhead's obstreperous and condescending manner of rehearsing, Mr. Cobb's introverted and monosyllabic approach to his role, and Lee Strasberg's well-meant but to me vague stage directions I felt utterly lost." Still, Bankhead wins hands down as the chief villain. "The lady was too much of a lady for the part," Mrs. Gottlieb quoted Odets as saying. "And when she realized this in rehearsal, the fireworks backstage topped any fireworks I'd written for onstage." Odets later told Ward Morehouse "of the night Lee J. Cobb broke the kitchen table in half as his answer to Tallulah's command to 'speak faster.' " Schildkraut wrote, "Had I ever lost my temper, even for a few minutes, I think I would have killed her."

This kind of characteristic backstage idiocy would not have amounted to much—might even have been taken as the familiar publicity game—if it had not helped to kill the play. *Clash by Night* opened at the Belasco on December 27, 1941, twenty days after the attack on Pearl Harbor, which no reviewer mentioned but which must have influenced their reactions to what they took as a trivial play. The reviews were mostly unfavorable, treating the play simply as a sordid triangle; the political overtones were scarcely mentioned. There was talk of salary cuts for the performers, other strategems to keep the play going, but it was only talk. The play closed on February 7, 1942, after forty-nine performances. *Variety* reported that *Clash* had been making enough money to keep running, that Odets had almost persuaded Rose to keep it open, but that "the mutual hatred society of Tallulah Bankhead, star of the play, and Billy Rose, its producer, prevailed." Miss Bankhead wrote, "Never did a final curtain fall on a more relieved actress." Billy Rose, who had told Lucius Beebe that he had produced the play because "I always was a fool for words that tinkle, and Odets can make words tinkle for me," sent a smoked turkey and a bottle of champagne to the reviewers who had panned the play with this note: "Having asked you to sit before one turkey, permit me to send you another."

Clash was eventually (1952) made into a movie, but its theatrical life came to an end that February. Odets had cause to regret the passing of the Group.

Clash by Night is a sordid triangle—from the reviewers' standpoint—only because it deals with working-class characters during a sticky summer on Staten Island. Otherwise, it follows the conventional plot of the erring wife, the jealous husband, the fatal ending. Mae Wilenski, bored, hot, tired, spends two scenes trying not to give in to the attractions of Earl Pfeiffer (minimal from the audience point of view), succumbs in I, 3, and is discovered at the end of the act. Retribution comes in Act II. The weaknesses of the play on that level are that it is heavy with exposition ("How old is the baby now . . . ?") and that the presence of Mae and Earl in the house, however convenient for the scene writer, seems farfetched after Act I. Two things—the temptation scene in II, 2, and the setting for the murder (the projection booth where Earl works)—are indications that Odets had something more than the standard triangle in mind.

Once again, Odets sets his play against a background of economic deprivation—Jerry loses his job on the "pro-jeck," Joe is on a three-day week, Peggy cannot find work as a teacher—but his customary setting is less believable than usual; men were dropped from WPA projects in the New York area in the summer of 1941, but with a booming construction industry a jobless Jerry is unlikely. The historical accuracy of the economic situation is finally not important. It is clear that the Depression playwright in Odets could not allow him to let loose of poverty as a motive, but that is not his real subject. *Clash* is another step in the way laid out by *Rocket to the Moon* and *Night Music;* the riches his characters lack can be found in some odd metaphors that turn up in the play ("A blondie mother an' a blondie girl—that's money in the bank!" says Jerry; "you've got a heart of gold, Peg, but it can't be cashed," says Mae). With these money-love phrases a bridge is made to the central subject, the insufficiency of the relationships (marriage, love affair, friendship) among the characters and the resulting sense of homelessness. "But I can't sleep," says Earl; it is not class guilt that keeps him awake—as in the early Odets monologue—but " 'Cause I'm always outside looking in!" Jerry's father plays a song which Jerry describes as "about the little old house, where you wanna go back, but you can't find out where it is no more," and Jerry longs for the world of the snowy house on Christmas cards. Unlike the Matthew Arnold poem which gives the play its title, *Clash* finds little comfort in love—at least for its central characters. It stays "on a darkling plain."

The personal failure of both Jerry and Earl stems from the fact that, as Vince says of the drunk with a marriage problem like Jerry's, "No manhood in the boy!" Jerry is like a child throughout the play, condescended to by both Mae and Earl; his image is the teddy bear in I, 4, to which he is specifically compared and which cries *"Momma, Momma"* as the act curtain comes down. Earl, too, is an aging boy ("A lot of bluster and then a boyish grin," says Joe), distantly reminiscent of some of Odets's younger heroes, but pushily desperate for attention and quick to lapse into self-pity ("Who gives a damn what I do or where I go?"). Neither of them fits Mae's dream of "big, comfortable men," like the Pennsylvania politician who was once her lover and who gave her "confidence." Earl and Mae try to reassure one another, but it is clear that their love is doomed before Jerry chokes Earl to death. Not that Mae's idea of a man is quite trustworthy for all her Pennsylvania memories and her proper (from the playwright's point of view) evaluation of Joe. Her challenge to Jerry's masculinity in I, 4 and his failure ("I didn't intend to go in your room at all," she says to Earl. "But you see . . . he didn't stop me") are straight out of the sentimental pop culture which is presumably smothering all three of them.

It is here, not in their financial difficulties, that Odets wants to make his main social point, although the running allusion to installment buying is an attempt to hook the two together. According to Joe, in his big speech in II, 2, the three main characters and "millions like them" are "clinging to a goofy dream—expecting life to be a picnic. Who taught them that? Radio, songs, the movies—" It is true that Mae says she enjoys "a good picture now and then," and both "Avalon" and "The Sheik of Araby" function in the play, calling up visions of a happy land and a romantic lover. Still, it is Odets, the social critic, not Odets, the playwright, who lays the blame for their discontent on the doorstep of the popular arts. That corruption is assumed in the play, not dramatized; at best, it emerges through allusion. Certainly, Odets intends the last scene in the projection booth, with the customary happy-ending movie playing off-stage, to pull the triangle and its presumed origins together.

Odets goes farther than that. "Part of the theme of this play is about how men irresponsibly wait for the voice and strong arm of Authority to bring them to life, to shape and working discipline," Odets said in the *Times* piece. "So can come fascism to a whole race of people." In Joe's big speech, it is a short step from false dreams to disillusionment and from there to a "Tricky Otto . . . with a forelock and a mustache" who will lead the deluded into horror. It is this part that Vince, Jerry's uncle, plays in *Clash*. "A man hits his wife and it is the first step to fascism!" says Carp in *Golden Boy*. A joke there, it becomes serious in *Clash*, for it is Vince who suggests that Jerry "give 'er the whip," who pushes his nephew to murder Earl. Odets makes Vince personally and politically unsavory. He is a bum, a cadger of drinks, a Peeping Tom, a pious pornographer; he is also an anti-Semite, a Coughlinite ("A great man said it, social justice for all"), an America-Firster, a religio-political fanatic. Odets called him "a sniveling, cunning little local Fascist". He is also a kind of bush-league Iago in II, 2, tempting Jerry to violence, and, as the stage directions say, a "devil" to Joe's "angel" in a struggle for Jerry's soul. "But you sit around an' nobody tells you what to do," laments Jerry in I, 4, for all the world like one of the irresponsible men in the Odets quotation at the head of this paragraph. Until Vince tells him. This development is somewhat obscured by the fact that suddenly in the last scene Odets gives Jerry a change of heart (an offstage priest on an offstage subway) which reduces the death of Earl to a misunderstanding.

When *Clash* first opened in Detroit, Russell McLaughlin complained that Joe and Peggy "appear sometimes to have wandered in from another play"—another Odets play, obviously, since they move into the mandatory positive position before the final curtain. At first, Joe is the usual Odetsian reluctant lover, unwilling to risk marriage when the funds are low. By I, 4, he is ready to marry, but Peggy, appalled by what she has learned of the marriage of Jerry and Mae, has new fears of her own. Joe's big speech persuades her that they at least have a chance for a happy marriage for they know "the anti-picnic facts . . . that Paradise begins in responsibility." Mae gives them her blessing. Joe is obviously necessary to this play as a balance to Vince and a voice to express the connection among the themes, but the Joe-Peggy plot, as Gerald Rabkin pointed out, is "in no way logically connected" to the triangle plot, is in fact the old "Marxist-redemption metaphor" with its structural support pulled away.

John Anderson followed his very negative review of *Clash*

with a second article on the play. One of the more perceptive of the daily critics, Anderson pointed out that the "neurotic intensity" in some of the scenes was "nothing more or less than effective theatricalism." Although meant as pejorative criticism, this seems to me a recognition of one of Odets's virtues, his creation of individual scenes emotionally appropriate to the genre in which he is working—this time the jealousy triangle. Anderson went on to say, "Odets simply tries for extra value, to put his work on a higher level, by the assumption that his inner meaning, beneath the externals of his work, has depth and significance," and it is here that the critic went wrong. As Roman Bohnen thundered in a letter to the New York *Times*, "Maybe emotional security has no connection with social stability throughout the world. Maybe a vulnerability for fascism does not appear in all countries for current environmental reasons," dismissing the *maybe-no* as he went. Odets's problem in *Clash* is not that his "inner meaning" lacks significance. That personal and political dislocation have the same roots is an important statement and a search for those roots is a major theme. To see popular culture as cause rather than symptom is a recurrent Odets mistake, but not one to lessen the ambitiousness of intention in *Clash*. The failure in the play is that this time Odets's parable is only fitfully interesting in itself and that it never successfully embodies the theme. The "inner meaning" remains outer, depends on Joe's explicative sermon for its existence.

XIV. "Why do they keep giving the Devil all the good tunes?"

T HE WAR WAS a difficult time," Clifford Odets told Seymour Peck. "They wouldn't take me for anything." An arthritic condition presumably kept him from active service, and he was turned down when he wanted to work on a *Winged Victory* kind of show involving a destroyer. "I was a premature anti-Fascist." That last line has a slightly false ring to it, although the ridiculous charge of premature anti-Fascism was real enough in the late 1940's. In any case, there was no war service for the playwright.

Odets's one notable contribution to the war effort was his adaptation of Konstantin Simonov's *The Russians*. The play was immensely popular in Russia where, as Marc Slonim said in *Russian Theater*, it "made millions of spectators laugh and cry." The Moscow Art Theater production "toned down the pathos of the play in order to stress sacrifice and patriotism as natural manifestations of Russian organic heroism." In an edition of the USSR Embassy *Information Bulletin* published just before the play opened in Washington, K. Borisov, who called the play "nobly modest," proclaimed that "truth is its principal hero." Such a play must have seemed the perfect export to the Soviet government, the proper seal to place on the Allied bond. In England, Tyrone Guthrie directed the Old Vic Company in his adaptation of the play. Here, the Theatre Guild presented

151

Odets's "American Acting Version" called *The Russian People*. There is no indication in Lawrence Langner's *The Magic Curtain* that the Russians had anything to do with the production, but Odets's later complaint to Michael J. Mendelsohn that "a Soviet governmental order" prohibited changes in the script implies a closer connection than Langner's condescending dismissal of the Maxim Litvinovs suggests. Langner's account of a cast party given by the Soviet Embassy provided the ambassador with tired-businessman tastes in theater and depicted his wife, Ivy, as a writer trying to peddle a movie script. It was the Guild, Langner said, which saw the play as "a good documentary picture of the kind of courageous fighting which was being done by the Russians with their backs against the wall" and which "felt that it might be of great value in making everyone alive to the need for stiffening the war effort."

Noble sentiments aside, Simonov's play is a standard flagwaver, very like so many American war movies, with poster-thin characters and set heroic and villainous bits; Lillian Hellman's *North Star* (1943) is an apt comparison. Langner knew this, of course. When the show was in rehearsal in Washington, the Guild sent Stella Adler (then Mrs. Harold Clurman) to assist her husband, and this message came back from the stage manager: "I wish you'd come down at once, Lawrence, Harold Clurman is rehearsing some of the actors on the stage for psychology, while Stella is rehearsing the others in the cellar underneath the stage, and telling them to play it for melodrama." Langner's comment: "Stella in the cellar wasn't so wrong after all." After two weeks in Washington, the play opened at the Guild Theatre in New York on December 29, 1942. The reviews are a study in the conflict between allegiance and aesthetics. With our Russian allies fighting so desperately, how could an American critic hurt their cause by hating their play? Never have so many critics tried so hard to be nice. There were two kinds of reviews: those that said the Russian front is great, therefore the play must be good, and those that said the Russian front is great, but the play is bad. Burton Rascoe, the harshest in the second group, wrote in his New York *World-Telegram* review: "The Russian People is not a tribute to the Russian people; it is a libel on them. It is almost a burlesque of the old ten-twenty-thirty melodrama." The play ran for thirty-nine performances and was almost certainly not instrumental in launching the second front.

In an interview in the *Information Bulletin* quoted above, Odets said, "I did not write the play, in any sense. I haven't changed the basic structure or the plot one whit. I merely tried to transpose it into clear and vital theatrical English." This is a muted version of what he said later to Mendelsohn, "Well, it's such a bad play; I shouldn't like to be responsible for it." He could make no changes at all, he said, until Ivy Litvinov got him permission to do some real rewriting, but by then it was too late. In the Theatre Collection of the New York Public Library there are typescripts of several different versions of the play which provide an opportunity to see how the adaptation developed. One, called *Men of Russia*, translated by Harris Moss, is presumably the literal translation from which Odets worked. It came to the library from someone at the Guild as did two almost identical Odets scripts, very similar to the one by Moss. A third Odets script, which came from the playwright himself, shows Odets beginning to burrow out from under the Simonov original; it is very like the version published in *Seven Soviet Plays* (1946). Odets did invent or alter business occasionally (in the expositional I, 1, Vasili bursts in, gun in hand, instead of sleeping in the backroom until time for his entrance), but the plot, the characters, the scenes remain the same. The greatest changes are in the language. A single example should serve—a speech by the hero's mother, recalling his gumption as a boy:

Moss version: I should think so. Good Lord . . . Everyone was always complaining to me about his pranks. And I'd say "Catch him. If you catch him I'll box his ears and if you don't then he'll escape scot free, and it's his luck."

Early Odets version: I should say so! Good Lord, always complaints about his pranks. "So catch him," I'd say. "I'll box his ears if you catch him. If you don't, he gets away."

Published Odets version: I should say so! He ran like the wind! He swam like a fish! He stole gooseberries, ate pancakes, kissed the girls! I should say so!

In the first instance, Odets simply tried to make the lines easier to speak; in the second he attempted to create the generalized all-Russian boy intended by the original speech. For the most part, his verbal additions leaned toward such specificity. Arthur Pollock, on the basis of nothing but a fondness for Russian movies, decided in his review that Clurman and Odets were to blame for the elements in the play that sound "like good American theater corn." Odets did occasionally add schmaltz on his own, as in III, 3, where Vasin, the old Tsarist officer, before he dies so bravely, answers the "Who's this?" over the dead sergeant with "Some Russian mother's son . . ." But the death scene is Simonov's, and so is the love story that Pollock distrusted, and so, apparently, are lines like "Old man, do you know you can make a man cry?" which the hero speaks when the veteran of the Russo-Japanese War volunteers to fight. Discredit where discredit is due, after all—*The Russian People* is more Simonov than Odets.

"Five years ago, the times cruelly out of joint, I went to Hollywood to recoup the small fortune the Group Theatre cost me in the last two years of its fervent life," Odets wrote in an article called "On Coming Home" in the New York *Times* (July 25, 1948). The bitter tone of the piece was more than the usual Odets back-from-Hollywood invective. The first investigation of Hollywood by the House Un-American Activities Committee had begun in October 1947, and the Hollywood Ten had been cited for contempt on November 27; almost immediately, the studio brass began to run scared and blacklists blanketed the town. In 1948, Hollywood was a good place for Odets to be coming from; in 1943, it had been the only place to go. After the failures of *Night Music* and *Clash by Night* and with a Simonov adaptation as his only weapon in the war, Odets was ready to head west again. "I hadn't made a living in the theater," he later told Ward Morehouse. "I was married and wanted to raise a family."

Odets married Bette Grayson on May 14, 1943, and not long after that, financed by John Garfield, he moved to Hollywood where he stayed for most of the next five years. The family came—a daughter, Nora, in 1945, and then a son, Walt

Whitman—and he had no trouble feeding them. He is quoted in *Variety* as saying that his income ran into six figures in his last year in Hollywood. Not that physical well-being implies spiritual ease. His letters to Alfred Stieglitz indicate his distaste for the work he was doing, a distress that was to explode into public statements on his return to New York. For two of his years in Hollywood, he told Morehouse, he worked as a trouble shooter for RKO. He wrote a number of scripts, some of which—*Sister Carrie* and a life of George Gershwin, for instance—were never produced. "I took my filthy salary every week and rolled an inner eye around an inner landscape," he said in the *Times* article. "Hollywood is a bon-bon town," he told Morehouse; "it's a taffy pull, and you get your financial awards from the taffy pulling." The taffy he pulled included not only *Deadline at Dawn* (1946) and *Humoresque* (1947), but *None But the Lonely Heart* (1944), which he directed as well as wrote. As Steve says in *Night Music,* "My mouth'll hang me yet."

"I enjoy his stentorian convictions and the courage he has to emphatically proclaim his everchanging beliefs," wrote Cary Grant of Clifford Odets. Stentorian the convictions may occasionally have been, but—on the evidence of *None But the Lonely Heart,* in which Grant starred as Ernie Mott—it was the circumstances more than the beliefs that had changed. Although Manny Farber decided that the film was a failure, he did detect a "daring and important movie subject . . . the theme of lonely hearts and social decay," which puts *None But* in the line that runs from *Rocket to the Moon* to *Clash by Night.* The plane passing over at the end of the film says "Wake up!" to Ernie, capping a conversion that puts the hero in the even older Odets line reaching back to Ralph in *Awake and Sing!* Although it was Grant who initiated the film, the hero of Richard Llewellyn's successful 1943 novel would seem less attractive to the actor than to Odets. Llewellyn's Ernest Verdun Mott, with a father dead in the First World War, is a boy of nineteen, a victim of sorts, just beginning to make his way in the world, wanting the best of everything and discovering that it is hard to get. With Grant in the part, Ernie becomes older, more sure of himself, "no longer pimpled or puerile" as *Time* put it. More important—and it is one of the weaknesses of the film—the self-indulgent, self-pitying adolescent becomes conventionally good, a characteristic that is repetitively dramatized from his giving the beggar his pack of cigarettes at the beginning to his rescuing the murderous Jim Mordinoy from the night-club fire near the end. This Ernie probably has as much to do with Grant's image as a star as it does with the ideational thrust of the film.

Not that that thrust is obscure. The emphasis throughout is on the squalor rather than the vitality of Ernie's slum street; by making Ma a penny-grabber, Odets suggests that existence here depends on a hierarchy of victimization. Ernie's distaste for his Ma's shop is emblematic of his attempt to dissociate himself from society as a whole. "Peace! That's what us millions want—" he says to Ma, "without having to snatch it from the smaller dogs. Peace—to be not a hound and not a hare." Ma says, "Won't find nothing in this world like that," and since Ernie is forced to agree he decides to "travel with the hounds!" He joins Jim's gang, but learns—from the beating of Ike Weber, the fear of Ada, the death of Ma—that his was a wrong choice, that he must "Fight with the men who'll fight for a human way of life." This line follows the injunction of Henry Twite, who sounds like Detective A. L. Rosenberger, "So if there's a better world to be made, you young ones will have to make it." Twite, a pale image of the interesting character in the novel, not much more really than an eccentric turn for Barry Fitzgerald, is never very clearly a mentor for Ernie in the film although he does have a way of looming up out of the fog when Ernie needs someone to talk to. For Manny Farber, the scene in Ike's shop is an example of Nazi brutality, a likely enough reading in the light of those planes at the end of the film. The Odets gangster (Jim) seems to have moved from capitalist figure to Nazi figure. At one point in the published screenplay, Ernie tells Ike that if a war comes he will not fight; although this passage is not in the finished film, it is still clear that Odets wants his character to move not only from separation to community, but from pacifism to a just war. When Leila S. Rogers went Red-hunting, she cited *None But the Lonely Heart* as a shocking example of a film which "takes time out for a bit of propaganda preachment whenever Director Clifford Odets . . . felt the urge." Odets wrote in a letter to *Time:* "I get damn tired of hearing crackpots here and in Washington constantly ascribing anything really human in films to the Communists alone. Why do they keep giving the Devil all the good tunes?" To support a war already in progress hardly seems a startling propaganda operation.

As a film, *None But* is in no way technically innovative. Using sets by Mordecai Gorelik and music by Hanns Eisler, Odets went for mood shots designed to suggest the separateness of the characters more than the physical fact of London. Sometimes Eisler's music is oppressively intrusive as in the scene in which the canary dies, and Odets's visual symbols—the grille door closed between Ernie and Ada—can be very corny. Although James Agee thought the film overwritten and the camera work too lush, he puts his finger on the real merit of the film which, in typical Agee fashion, he saw as Odets's "faith in and love for people." What he meant is that the movie, like Odets's plays, is filled with interesting types, some with only a single scene to play. It is true that one is more likely to remember Ma (Ethel Barrymore) putting on her hat or Dad Prettyjohn (Roman Bohnen) reaching for a package of cigarettes or the old lady with the canary than the exact nature of Ernie Mott's conversion.

The other two Odets films of the 1940s are of minimal interest. *Deadline at Dawn,* directed by Harold Clurman, is a thriller distantly based on the William Irish novel (1944) of the same name. It concerns a sailor and a girl and their need to solve a murder before dawn so that he can escape being charged with the crime and get back to his base on time. They are helped by a philosophic cab driver who turns out to have been the murderer and who finally confesses for the sailor's sake. If the film does nothing else, it provides, in the person of the cab driver, an anthology of Odets lines past and future: "But Steve Brody took a chance!" *(Paradise Lost);* "it's beautiful to struggle for the human possibilities" (a variation on Rosenberger); "happiness is no laughing matter" *(The Big Knife).*

Except for the scene of the irate father and the birthday fiddle, there is almost nothing of Fannie Hurst in *Humoresque,* the film supposedly based on her story (1919) about the Jewish violin virtuoso. The movie, directed by Jean Negulesco, is, as *Newsweek* said, "a certified tear jerker, for the matinee trade;" it has one of the most protracted suicide sequences on film, as

Joan Crawford contemplates the inviting sea while John Garfield's violin (actually Isaac Stern's) sings sadly in the background. Since the film is primarily the story of a tough, cocky violinist who fights his way through the Depression to success, glimpses of Odets may be seen in the screenplay, for which he and Zachary Gold share credit. "Are you a prize fighter?" asks a girl who may have seen *Golden Boy*. Most of the good lines go to Oscar Levant, who claimed that he wrote his own lines; some of them are plainly Odets, in rhythm and in content: "You're suffering from the old American itch. You want to get there fast and you don't want to pay for the ride." Artistically, the movie was of no importance to Odets's career; more practically, it marked his first association with Jerry Wald, the producer for whom he was to make his last films.

There were outer as well as inner landscapes for Odets in Hollywood during the 1940s. A well-known art collector (Modigliani, Utrillo, Soutine, most of all Klee), he began to play at being an artist himself. He once turned out 150 watercolors in as many days—or so Earl Wilson reported in 1947 at the time of Odets's show at J. B. Neumann's gallery in New York. Although it is difficult to judge by a black-and-white newspaper reproduction, "The Cats of Belfonte," reproduced on the cover of the magazine section of *PM*, looks like a cross between Klee and kindergarten; the accompanying story described it as having "the muted colors of a dull, gray day." There was another show in 1948 and six of his watercolors were in an amateur show that the Philadelphia Museum of Art put on in October 1952. Less art than avocation.

XV. *"Half-idealism is the peritonitis of the soul"*

CLIFFORD ODETS once sulked through a party because his wife, Luise Rainer, insisted on taking advantage of the servants' night off to recreate a Viennese Sunday evening, serving the guests herself. The next day she explained his anger: "he said this wasn't Vienna, it was Hollywood and in Hollywood one had servants; otherwise, why come here?" Ella Winter told the story in *And Not to Yield* as an example "of the curious values of the movie colony," but, if it is true, it is an even better example of the curious attitude of Odets toward those values.

Odets once tried to differentiate between two kinds of play-writing, mere "fabrication" and something with which the words "creative" and "art" might be used. The second, which "begins always with the premise of expressing a personal state of being," often starts with an imprecise feeling. For instance, "all his life he [the imaginary playwright] has wanted to be a good and true man, but recently has understood in himself an ignoble tendency to personal and selfish success." If Miss Winter's story is a ludicrous example of the "ignoble tendency," *The Big Knife* may have begun in unwelcome self-understanding. There had been glimmers earlier, of course, or there could have been no *Golden Boy*.

The Big Knife was produced by Dwight Deere Wiman, in association with Odets and Lee Strasberg, who directed it. Written in 1948, the play was extensively revised before it reached New York. Two characters—a publicity man and a business manager—were cut from the script, as were a great many lines; a typescript of an earlier version of the play in the Theatre Collection of the New York Public Library indicates that there was no major change in the central movement or intention of the script.

There is a two-line exchange early in *Knife* in which Charlie Castle defends his wife against the political insinuations of a self-righteous columnist; a little later Marcus Hoff refers to Marion's "reprehensible politics;" in the last act, commenting on world revolution, Hank Teagle says, "Here, of course, that platitude carries with it the breath of treason." It is only in these few lines that Odets acknowledged the troubled, frightened Hollywood on which he had temporarily turned his back. It was another, an earlier Hollywood he was after, one in which the moral climate—which is to say, the economic climate—prepared the way for the collapse that followed the contempt citations for the Hollywood Ten. *Variety*, in a favorable review of the New Haven opening, January 26, 1949, predicted that Odets would be criticized for his assault on Hollywood. That criticism came before the show was out of Boston, the second and last city on its pre-Broadway schedule. Hedda Hopper, after whom Odets's gossip columnist might well have been modeled, attacked obliquely through the play's star; in a column datelined February 3, she reported:

> "The Big Knife," Clifford Odets' play which pokes fun at Hollywood, with John Garfield starred, didn't get cheers out of town. Serves Garfield right. This town was very good to him, and since this is the way he shows his gratitude, perhaps he deserves a failure.

Both Elinor Hughes and Elliot Norton, neither of whom had written an enthusiastic first review of the play, devoted Sunday columns to a defense of Odets and Garfield. "It all has a familiar ring," wrote Miss Hughes, "this defensive-aggressive attitude of alternately cajoling and browbeating any writer or player who presumes to criticize the motion picture industry." Once the play opened in New York (at the National, February 24), Hollywood no longer needed to voice its protests; theater critics sprang to its defense. The general tenor of the reviews was that Hollywood was not all that bad and that, as another *Variety* reviewer put it, Odets was "the champ sorehead of show business" for taking all that money and not being properly humble about it. Perhaps because the reviews had praised the production, more likely because Garfield was, after all, a movie star, *Knife* lasted for 108 performances. It closed on May 28.

In 1954, Sam Wanamaker, one of the American theatrical political exiles in England, staged the play in London to indifferent notices. Ironically, by that time, Hollywood was ready for *The Big Knife*. The film industry had begun to take a jaundiced view of itself shortly after Odets's play opened in New York—in *Sunset Boulevard* (1950) and *The Bad and the Beautiful* (1952). Readers of the *New Yorker*, through Lillian Ross's interview with Louis B. Mayer, had already learned that Hollywood producers cry. By 1955, when the movie version of *The Big Knife* was released, it was already old hat. Odets, who had made his political peace with the industry by then, wrote an article in the New York *Times* which was little more than a puff for the picture, calling it the best movie yet made from his plays. There was unintentional self-condemnation in that praise, for the movie—remarkably faithful to the Odets original—was excessively dull, getting very little of the dramatic vitality that a reading of the play suggests can be found in individual characters and scenes, if not in the play as a whole. It was that now-and-again vitality that attracted the attention of the few reviewers who responded favorably to the off-Broadway revival, directed by Peter Bogdanovich, for a nine-week run at the Seven Arts Theatre, November 11, 1959. That was the last professional production in New York.

The Big Knife has been copyrighted as *A Winter Journey*. In explaining the title change, Odets said that the latter indicated "a difficult passage in one's life;" the former, "a force that moves against people." This suggests, as a number of reviewers insisted, that Odets was more interested in condemning the outside forces than examining his central character's complicity in his own destruction. Since the attack on Hollywood is a vicious one, there is something almost too dainty in the attempts to step away from it, made by Odets in a number of post-Boston interviews. "This new play of mine is about certain moral facts, written as objectively as possible," he told Ward Morehouse. "It's not necessarily about Hollywood." Despite the ambiguity in those lines—his saying *I didn't do it* in so reasoned a way—I believe his insistence about the play's main subject: "it's essentially about a man trying to keep his integrity against corrupting outside combinations." It is here, in fact, that the problem of the play lies and it can best be seen through a comparison with *Golden Boy.* "Does the man in your book get out of here?" Charlie asks Hank, whose hero is a man like Charlie. "Where does he go? What, pray tell, does he do? Become a union organizer?" This oblique reference to Frank Bonaparte and the other possibility in *Golden Boy,* spoken (and written, too, I suspect) by a man who can find no way out, is more than a bitter nod to the earlier play. Marion defines Charlie's difficulties in the terms that Mr. Bonaparte uses on Joe: "Your sin is living against your own nature. You're denatured—that's your sin!" Charlie Castle, then, is another Joe Bonaparte, but we meet him late in the game, after he has killed a little girl hit-and-run, less clean than Joe's match with the Drop. He has already destroyed his other self, Charlie Cass: "A hot-head with clenched fists and a big, yammering mouth!" The Charlie we meet is defensively charming, unwilling to risk commitment even to the wife he loves; he is a drunk and a bored sensualist, almost indifferent to the willing flesh that falls his way. Early in the play, Patty Benedict, the columnist, reminds him that when he first came to Hollywood he would talk about nothing but FDR. "I believed in FDR," he says and when she asks for his current belief, he answers, "What we had for lunch—roast beef, rare!" This exchange marks the distance between the successful movie star and the hopeful youth who believed not only in political and social possibilities, but in professional ones, in himself and his art.

One of the weaknesses of the character, as so many of the critics complained, is that we are forced to take that idealism on faith. It is in the play—in his self-pity, in Marion's regret, in the mouths of the other characters—but if an audience fails to accept it, the anguish is milked out of the play, is replaced by audience exasperation. The difficulty in accepting Charlie in the terms in which the play presents him is, strangely, a structural problem in the play itself. The melodramatic plots as well as extra-dramatic Odets phrases like "to keep his integrity" imply that he still has integrity to keep, that Charlie Castle may be where Joe Bonaparte is in Act I of *Golden Boy*, still able to turn away. Marion seems to assume he is, at least until the end of Act II, and the "can this marriage be saved" plot appears to hinge on his ability not to sign a fourteen-year contract. The contract plots peters out in Act I and so does the teasing, mystery-story plot about what really happened the night of the accident. By then, the new tease is under way: will Dixie Evans talk and will Charlie conspire in murder to keep her quiet? When the confrontation comes in the last act, it is neither the triumph of melodrama (the villains are not routed) nor an Odets conversion. Charlie learns not how to live, but that his choices are death or the corruption that he has rushed to embrace, protesting all the way. The manipulative nonsense in the play almost hides the real plot, the movement from Charlie's "I can change" in Act I to his "I realize what I am" in III, 2. "One begins to ask oneself the startling question: Does Charlie really hate Hollywood?" wrote Harold Clurman in *Lies Like Truth.* "Isn't he in fact hellishly attached to it?" Of course, he is and that is what makes the character interesting. Unless we assume, as Clurman apparently did, that Odets wants to make a simple moral point about the corruption of the innocent, we can see *The Big Knife* as the story of a man who at once loves and hates his success. "Stop torturing yourself, Charlie—don't resist!" says Hank. "Your wild, native idealism is a fatal flaw in the context of your life out here. Half-idealism is the peritonitis of the soul—America is full of it! Give up and really march to Hoff's bugle call!" Charlie, who could let his best friend go to jail for him and then sleep with the friend's wife, stops short of murder for his career's sake, but in facing that problem he discovers the truth in Coy's "the day you first scheme . . . you marry the scheme and the scheme's children." Unable to make the peace Hank suggests, he kills himself, having said earlier, jokingly, "Hank—be my Horatio." And so Hank is: "He . . . killed himself

. . . because that was the only way he could live. You don't recognize a final . . . a final act of faith . . . when you see one." The play does not end on this halting (the elipses are Odets's) affirmation, but on Marion's "Help! . . . Help! . . . Help!! . . . Help!!!"

Back in 1936, Arthur Pollock did a Sunday column on the radical writers in Hollywood in which he printed the defenses of Odets and John Howard Lawson and commented "that the general tragedy of American life is played out in Hollywood with a concentration not often found elsewhere in the country." That line sounds like a preview of *The Big Knife*—at least in its intentions. Odets, as usual, wanted more than a simple story; he was reaching for the "general tragedy." He told *Variety* that he chose the Hollywood locale because it "happened to be the suitable large community that I knew best," that Detroit or Pittsburgh would have done as well. "I deliberately placed particular characters in a particular environment," he said in the *Herald Tribune* interview quoted earlier, "hoping that they'd raise themselves to symbols. The moral dilemma is purposely exaggerated to the nth degree." The authenticity he talked about in *Variety* and the exaggeration in the *Herald Tribune* suggest a conflict of method; more likely, as is usually the case with Odets interviews, each is a response to the criticism that has most recently annoyed him. Both are ways of saying that the play's significance is greater than the playwright's personal anger. The play tries to make the jump from Hollywood as microcosm. One step is the familiar Odetsian attack on movies, an echo from *Clash by Night:* "Don't they murder the highest dreams and hopes of a whole great people with the movies they make?" The most serious statement of the larger theme is in the conversation between Hank and Charlie in III, 1, in which the latter recalls coming back from the war only to find the same old society: "and we plunged ourselves, all of us, into the noble work of making the buck reproduce itself." Hank, seeing a world of unfulfilled promises, foresees "defeat, decay, depression and despair."

Both Charlie's destruction and the social point implicit in it are obscured not simply by excessive plotting but by the character actor's gallery in which the play takes place. The collection of victims and victimizers that Odets brings together in his attack on Hollywood has a way of upstaging Charlie and Marion and good gray Hank. Some of them, like Hoff, are pure caricature; others, like Nat, are little more than representative types. Theatrically, they are the best thing in the play. Hoff is a recognizable villain, all oily malevolence and egomania, but Odets makes something special of him by seeing him as a verbal construct, a convoluted pattern of speech which leads through incredible usage ("the vexing problems, so manifold, of the heat and toil of the day") and improbable metaphor ("I'm like a girl in a summer-time canoe—I can't say no!") always back to Hoff and the tears in *his* sacrifice; appropriately, in the last act, Charlie fights him by stopping the flow of his words. Smiley Coy is a machine, camouflaged in amiability, an unfeeling process—as the gin-rummy sequence in Act II shows—in which even the most casual line is part of a specific and probably ugly pattern. Nat is an even more interesting part of the corruption surrounding Charlie. Although he is a stereotypical good man, Jewish variety, and although he has his moment of glory in III, 2, slapping Hoff's sparkling water from his hand, he is Charlie's agent, constantly in touch with Hoff, destined to make $350,000 if Charlie signs the contract. In Act I, he promises Charlie to protect him from the trivial scripts that he has been filming; in Act III, he tries to softsoap Charlie into doing a musical with "is every picture you do a test of your integrity?" Dixie Evans is another Charlie Castle image; in her one scene, she bubbles enthusiastically, not realizing that she is powerless against forces which, in her case, Charlie represents.

Whatever the incidental virtues of *The Big Knife*, the play was finally caught by its biographical-historical context. Odets, slamming the Hollywood door behind him, was torn between scoring them off out there and writing a real study of the Charlie Castle dilemma. The play might have been stronger if Charlie had not committed suicide, but gone ahead and made that musical. Shortly before he died, Odets told Michael J. Mendelsohn: "At that time I had had California up to the neck and could never make peace with the place. Now I've learned to make peace with it."

XVI. *"a little realism is of the essence"*

THERE'S ONLY ONE trouble with 'The Country Girl.' It should be called 'Theater Piece.'" Clifford Odets passed this judgment on his play in an interview in the Philadelphia *Bulletin* just before the road company was to arrive in his old home town. He would continue to dismiss *Girl* as "a superficial play" until the end of his life; although certain creative things may have "crept into" the play, he said, it was written only out of a need to make money. "To Clifford Odets, 'The Country Girl' may be a pot-boiler . . ." wrote Brooks Atkinson. "But to most of us it is the best play Mr. Odets has written in years." Next only to *Golden Boy*—that one supposedly written to boil the Group's pot—*The Country Girl* was Odets's most successful play.

The idea for the play came to Odets while he was involved in the production of *The Big Knife,* he told an interviewer, but it was not until later, when Charles Coburn expressed an interest in returning to the stage, that he sat down and wrote it. Three drafts in sixteen days, he said. Although Coburn gave him the "psychological boost" he needed to write the play, he explained to Elliot Norton, the actor was too old for the protagonist's role as it finally took shape. In the fall of 1950 the producing team from *The Big Knife*—Dwight Deere Wiman, Lee Strasberg and Odets himself—put *Girl* into production. This time Odets was his own director. "He talks about the characters, rather than tries to demonstrate what the actors should do," said Forrest C. Haring, the company manager, commenting on Odets's practice as a director. Odets explained, "I almost feel that it is better not to have the actors know too much of the philosophical overtones of a play. The affinity of the actor to the part is far more important." Odets may have had his own directorial methods in mind in *Girl*, at least in the scene in which Bernie deflects Frank's "What does he mean?" by insisting that "the theatrical meaning is more important" and explaining the line in terms not of its content but of how the character uses it. After opening in Boston (October 24, 1950), the play moved on to the Lyceum in New York (November 10). The majority of the reviews were enthusiastic. Most of the critics pointed out that the playwright had turned from social criticism to "a plain, human story," as Atkinson put it. That hardly needed saying since it was implicit in reviews which devoted more space to the performers than to the play's content. The play ran for 235 performances. By the time it closed on June 2, 1951, it had been sold to the movies. A road company took the play on tour during the 1952-53 season.

The play was produced in London in 1952 under the title *Winter Journey*. For Odets, that name indicated "a difficult passage in one's life," which makes it more appropriate to *The Country Girl* than to *The Big Knife*, for which he first used it. There were changes other than the title in London—as the English acting edition indicates—but they were minor, involving substitutions for phrases and references that an English audience might have trouble grasping. The film version, which was released in 1954, altered the role of Frank Elgin for Bing Crosby, turning the actor into a musical performer. The play was revived in New York in 1966 (at the City Center) and in 1968. For the latter production, an ill-fated off-Broadway venture, an unidentified adapter had updated the play; it was again called *Winter Journey*. Most of the reviews of the two revivals found the play dated, an ironic fate for a "Theater Piece" presumably unhampered by the usual Odetsian topicality.

Robert Coleman, one of the few reviewers to pan the play, called it a "saga of the boozey, unreliable ham who gets another chance and makes good. The movies have done it a dozen times." His is an accurate description of the story of Frank Elgin although Odets tells it with a minimum of the sentimentality Coleman's phrasing implies. If the actor (it was Paul Kelly originally) who plays Elgin is talented enough, the supposedly improvisatory scene in I, 1, will establish the character that is—or was—an actor of consequence. It is the business of the Elgin plot to let the artist emerge from the frightened, beaten, sometimes drunken man whom we see on stage most of the time. Odets is better at presenting the latter than at charting the emergence. Frank's running away after the improvisation in the first scene establishes the depth of his self-doubt and his fear of rejection. His understandable distress on finding himself rehearsing a leading role after years on the skids is complicated by his image of himself as an easy-going, joking fellow. He even works up false exuberance for Georgie (I, 4), but she has been married to him too long to accept his moods at face value. More often he whines at her. He lets her relay his complaints, thus turning her into the grouch that he—the beaming boy—is afraid to be. His movement from beer (I, 4) to cough syrup that is twenty-two per cent alcohol (II, 1) to a real bender at the end of that scene is predictable to Georgie and to the audience if not to the other characters in the play. That "to the audience" may be a little hasty since critics as practiced as Richard Watts Jr. and John Mason Brown assumed that the audience sees through Bernie's eyes, but even though Odets feints trickily—by letting Georgie look out over the footlights at the end of I, 3, right after Frank's lies about her career—I find it difficult to imagine that with such familiar dramatic material the audience will fail to pick up the clues in the first two scenes and work from Georgie's point of view all the way through. Elgin may be explained more often than necessary in this far too expository play, but he remains an interesting creation. That does not mean that his last-scene success is acceptable within the play's own terms. All that happens in II, 2 is that Bernie ceases to fight Georgie and they become allies in trying to keep Frank on his feet; this combination apparently works the wonders we see in II, 3. Odets apparently had doubts of his own about that final scene. Uta Hagen (who played Georgie) told an interviewer that the play had five different endings before it got to New York and Odets said that the scene was written only four or five days before *Girl* opened on Broadway. He also called it "the best technical job I ever did," but I suspect that means simply that he made plausible-sounding an ending which came out of nothing but the conventions of Coleman's "boozey" saga.

Odets said that the "real interpretation" of the last scene lay with the audience, which is a way of saying that it is not a simple happiness-ever-after ending. It is a positive final curtain because Frank is in the middle of a professional triumph and because Georgie decides to stay with him, but she phrases her decision so tentatively that all the ugly, old possiblities still lurk around the stage. She is much more difficult to grasp as a character than Frank is. "I had one long old-fashioned cry out there," she says after the first dress rehearsal. "Just a country girl." The suggestion of simplicity, of lack of sophistication in the label is lost in the fact that she hangs it on herself; Frank's use of it in II, 1 ("But do I still have the country girl?") suggests that it is an old joke of theirs, the country girl carried off by the show-business city slicker. Insofar as it is a valid description of Georgie it suggests her directness and her solidity, but one of these has turned to indirection ("He's taught me to be a fish, to swim in any direction, including up, down and sideways") and the other is collapsing, if her desire to get out from under can be taken as genuine. Bernie says at the end that she is "steadfast. And loyal . . . reliable," but he has hardly proved himself a trustworthy observer of his fellowmen. Georgie was originally conceived as "a very destructive, bitchy woman,"° but as the play finally stands she is the chief sustaining force in Frank's life. It would be a mistake, however, to turn her into the cliché implicit in Harold Clurman's description of Frank as "a shattered man . . . who is restored to his pride and professional proficiency by the love of a patient and faithful wife." John Gassner, who called her a "corn-fed madonna," suspected that Odets had written Georgie "with the same ambivalence that Shaw brought to his Candida." That seems nearer the truth to me because the scenes between Frank and Georgie indicate that

°The phrase became "a destructive, emasculative woman" when Odets edited his *Theatre Arts* remarks for *13 Plays*, ed. Stanley Clayes and David Spencer, New York, 1962.

the lines and the gestures that she uses to shore him up are also the means to his collapse. Her impatient patience and her doubting faith have not restored him in fifteen years of marriage; it takes a last-act curtain to do that. If her complicity in the fall and rise of Frank is uncertain, it is even more difficult to understand what she wants for herself. Uta Hagen suggested why when she described Georgie as "a new sort of heroine in the theater—a woman who keeps her feelings to herself." Georgie does speak sharply on occasion and once she even slaps Bernie, but for most of the play she simply stands around, a restless earth mother, mocking her own role—as in her constant reference to herself as old. She insists that what she wants is "the fiesta of a quiet room" and "a modest job to buy the sugar for my coffee," but she has left Frank twice and returned each time because "He's a helpless child." That leaves her the sacrificing heroine that many of the reviewers saw in her, but Uta Hagen found more there. For her, Georgie also needs Frank: "He has been the center of her life for years. . . . She knows his weaknesses and fears and she could never stop thinking of him even if he went away."

The triangle in the play is difficult to take. Although Odets plants a few early lines (Bernie's angry, "I could almost love a woman like you" in I, 5), it is only the love-hate bromide of theater psychology that makes him suddenly kiss her in II, 2. Odets tries to give credibility to the action by letting Bernie describe himself as "a homeless man" and make a final pitch for Georgie with "You could be a home for me." The description seems accurate in retrospect, a familiar diagnosis for a character whom Walter Kerr called "an Odets standby: the biting, restless egocentric." In Georgie's reaction to the kiss ("To be so mad at someone you didn't even know . . . ?") there is the suggestion of a theme, using Bernie, which is much more important than the triangle plot itself. Although Frank and Georgie are more interesting characters than Bernie, it is through him that the play makes its most serious statement about the relations among human beings. He is so obtuse that he is almost incredible, but Odets uses that obtuseness not only to stretch out a tenuous plot, but to say something specific about the way we all invent the people with whom we are associated. "Mr. Dodd

. . . we had a town idiot when I was a child . . . he kept insisting that elephant's tusks come from piano keys." Like Georgie's town idiot, Bernie, who knew the piano keys of his own life before he saw the elephant's tusks of the Elgin marriage, tries to fit Frank and Georgie into preconceived roles. Frank is Bernie's father all over again, the alcoholic he did not save from the subway wheels. He denies the relationship with his "Don't call me son!" in I, 2 and affirms it with the same line, said this time "*Grinning,*" in I, 3. That his salvage operation is an attempt to rewrite his own family history is less important than the fact that his casting of Frank in the father role makes it impossible for him to see the man in reality. In the case of Georgie, whom he twice calls "Mrs. Dodd," Bernie's confusion is even more obvious. Having just extricated himself from a destructive marriage, he sees all women in the person of his ex-wife. This is clear in I, 3 when he moves with no apparent transition from Frank's alcoholism to Georgie and again, a few lines later, from her to a generalized *they.* "Women always think they understand their men, don't they?" he says in II, 1, arguing with Georgie, and the sentence defines his own inadequacy. At the beginning of the play, he defends the hiring of Frank with "a little realism is of the essence," and then proceeds straight through to II, 2 without looking squarely at anything that happens around him.

Odets has in the theatrical setting a perfect background against which to present the theme of willful blindness. He does make use of the truth-illusion ambiguity familiarly associated with the theater. Bernie, who directs on and off-stage, waits patiently for Frank's stage character to grow but will not wait two sentences for a glimpse of a Georgie not in his mental script about villainous women. Frank gets his lies about Georgie from his old hit *Werba's Millions* (and I expect Odets got that name from Werba's Brooklyn Theater, where Theatre Guild shows—*Marco Millions,* for instance—sometimes stopped in Odets's acting days). The most effective use of the theater, however, comes in the first scene in which Frank, reading for the role, improvises a scene with Bernie. Part the play in production, part *Werba's Millions,* the improvisation is dramatically a definition of Frank's sense of being menaced by Bernie and his good intentions ("Nobody wants your pity or your help!"). These are almost incidental attractions in the play, however, for the theater is not used consistently to strengthen either the dramatic or the thematic force of the play, and even the Bernie theme is finally peripheral to the rehabilitation and the marriage plots. As to the social overtones one expects in Odets, they are all but gone. "I never wrote a play that didn't tell a story," he said in *Theatre Arts*. "The only thing is that I usually verbalized the implications . . . things like what makes a man like Frank Elgin a drunkard." Perhaps the distance between "show business, trying hard to be theater," as Bernie calls the play within the play, and simple show business is that, in the former, the dramatist is clearly concerned with "implications" even if he does not verbalize them. Bernie's "theater" is not what Odets meant when he suggested the title "Theater Piece." That's show business.

XVII. *"There is idealism now in just survival!"*

THE FLOWERING PEACH, Clifford Odets's last play, began in 1953 as an idea for an opera with Aaron Copland. It was a play in the fall of 1954, when Robert Whitehead put it into production, but not the one that would finally reach New York. Odets was his own director, except—as he told Herbert Mitgang—when Martin Ritt (who played Shem) took over while he was rewriting. The play opened in Wilmington on November 11 and went on to Baltimore, Washington and Boston.

It arrived in the last city with a new second act, "performed here for the first time anywhere," Elinor Hughes reported, and a new Japheth, Mario Alcalde having replaced William Smithers in the role. It opened at the Belasco in New York on December 28. The reviews were friendly ones, giving the impression that the critics wanted to like the play more than they did. It was the family story, the echoes of *Awake and Sing!*, that most found appealing and they tended to dwell on Menasha Skulnik (Noah) more fondly than on the play itself. The Pulitzer Prize jurors, Oscar J. Campbell and Maurice Valency, chose *Peach* for the prize that year, but they were overruled by the Advisory Board which gave it to Tennessee Williams's *Cat on a Hot Tin Roof*. When the *Times* broke the story after Odets's death, it was confirmed by Campbell, who said, "Yes, we did pick 'The Flowering Peach.' It didn't get the prize. I haven't any idea why." That is as close as Odets ever came to a Pulitzer. The unprized play closed on April 23, 1955, after 135 performances. Although Louis Kronenberger printed an abridged version of *Peach* as one of *The Best Plays of 1954–55*, the complete play was never published. For the discussion that follows, I am using the typescript in the Theatre Collection of the New York Public Library. That version, in nine scenes, has no act designations; it was played in two acts in the New York production, the first-act curtain coming at the end of the fifth scene as the Flood begins.

"And Noah did according unto all that the Lord commanded him." In *Genesis* (7:5), any difficulties Noah may have had with himself or his family are conveniently hidden behind that sentence. A contemporary playwright is bound to worry about the old gentleman's credibility, particularly if, like Odets's Noah, he is a somewhat seedy patriarch, rather too given to drink. Odets, then, spends the first two scenes verifying Noah's vision and God's commandment. In scene I, God rejects Noah's excuses ("I'm too old . . . I ain't got the gizzard for it") and convinces him with a roll of thunder. In II, his doubting wife and sons are persuaded when the animals assemble. These two scenes are fairly broad Jewish family comedy and although Odets is supposed to have drawn Noah and his wife from an uncle and aunt in Philadelphia, they are much closer to vaudeville Jews than the Bergers in *Awake*. In a stage direction in II, Odets calls them "Noah and his troupe . . . assorted clowns and acrobats." It seems clear that what Odets wants to do, as so often in the earlier plays, is to work from generic stereotype (this time, two genres: the Jewish family play and the anachronistic Biblical comedy) to create a play that is at once serious and attractive in a familiar way. One difficulty with *Peach* is that the wispy Noah established in the first two scenes has to carry a heavy authoritarian burden before the play is finished.

The key figure in the serious play is Japheth, the younger son, for it is his quarrel with Noah that takes over the second act. His first antagonist, however, is God: "Someone, it seems to me, would have to protest such an avenging, destructive God!" Actually, it is Noah who first voices Japheth's complaint when in the opening scene he chides God: "You're talking a total de-

struction of the whole world an' this is something terrible—!"
Japheth decides not to board the ark, to make his protest by
dying with the rest of mankind. He walks out at the end of the
third scene but returns in IV—"for the family, not for God"—to
help finish the ark. But nothing—not his affection for his parents
nor his love for Rachel, his brother Ham's wife—can make him
decide to live. His quarrel is not resolved, but it ends abruptly
in V when Noah, his youth newly restored, knocks his son out
and has him carried on board. This lack of resolution makes the
Japheth-vs-God plot seem like a false start, a major theme carefully planted but arbitrarily cut away. Even so, it prepares in
two ways for the Noah-Japheth struggle. It defines Japheth, particularly in the scene with Rachel in V, as one who believes in
man rather than God. His metaphor about the roads—"men
crazy not to be alone or apart"—is a testimony not to an idealized future, but to man's attempts to reach beyond himself in
this world. For Noah, Japheth's refusal to obey God is the sign
of a bad son. He may seem to have the priorities turned around
in "Disrespect to a father is disrespect to God!" but in that
phrase he steps past Japheth's argument into the truth of their
situation. The theomachic protest is an image of the father-son
conflict.

Their first clash is comic (if not very funny)—an argument
over how *tiger* should be pronounced. Japheth's solution ("Fine,
Poppa, you say teeger and I'll say tiger") is a deceptively simple
one for the real points of contention between them can only be
solved with one person giving way to the other. The two
conflict plots concern a rudder for the ark (Japheth introduces
the possibility in the sentence following his teeger-tiger line)
and a bride for Japheth. The rudder quarrel is whether man or
God should guide the ark and Japheth wins in VII when, with
the ark slowly sinking after having hit a floating house, he
agrees to put them all in God's hands until Noah, tacitly admitting that God needs help, sends Japheth to fix the leak: "he'll
use his own judgment." In the wife-swapping plot, Japheth
wants Rachel rather than Goldie, whom Noah insists he marry,
and Ham would be happy to make the exchange, but Noah,
pleading ancient authority ("it stands in the books for a thousand years"), refuses to countenance the switch. His wife, Es-

ther, the practical foil to his rigidity, wants him to marry them. Dying, she pleads with him in VIII, but he remains enclosed in his righteousness: "First place, he won't permit such marriages, the God I know. And secondly, He won't let nothing happen to you, the God I know." Her death at the end of the scene teaches him that "Maybe you don't know Him . . . anymore," and he blesses the children: "Go better now every husband should kiss each wife, as Mother wanted."

These plots are merely contrivances to convey the basic quarrel between Noah and his son. That they represent the same thing is clear from an exchange in VI in which, following an argument over Goldie, Noah says, "Next I guess you'll start with the rudder?" Stated simply, their struggle is the standard generational one, the fight between the authoritarian father and the unyielding son, but its emotional force rests on the closeness of the two characters. "Where is Japheth?" asks a troubled Noah shortly after the curtain goes up and it is in Japheth's arms that he cries when Esther dies. The thematic strength of their conflict lies in the similarity of the two characters. Rachel's "you're just like your father" is a gentle way of affirming Shem's outcry in the middle of the boat-sinking scene—"you two fanatics!" Odets himself, in a stage direction, calls them "two outcasts in the more competent and fluent world," and he is careful in the play to differentiate them from the other brothers and even from Esther and the girls. Shem is a cartoon capitalist who wails *what am I without my money?!* but who recovers from the losses of IV to corner the manure market in VI, manufacturing "dried manure briquettes" to sell for fuel when the ark finally settles on not-very-dry land. Ham is the mocker, the drinker, always ready, out of an immediate, self-indulgent need, to do his older brother's bidding. "What can you build, coins one on top of another?" Esther asks Shem and then turns to Ham, "And you, what? A pile of empty bottles in a back yard?" At this point Japheth, difficult though he may be, is building the ark. The qualities that Rachel finds in Noah and Japheth—"love, wrath, gentleness and all"—are positive ones. They are builders and dreamers, odd idealists who are strangely egocentric in their otherness. That Japheth is his father's own son is clear from this exchange about the rudder:

Noah: God never said we should steer the ark!
    Tomorrow first thing you'll take it off!
Japheth: *(Temper slipping)* And God didn't tell
    you to invent the hoe and the rake and
    yet you did!"
Noah: *(Flatly)* I was a youngster then—what
    did I know?

Walter Kerr complained that the sons "are a graceless lot" and
was outraged to discover that "they possess the true key to
man's happiness and that Noah has been far too impatient with
them," but I suspect that it was a case of Skulnik's likableness
working against the script. Surely, Noah, too, is a little "graceless," using a rigid God to hold the young in line but letting the
infinite inflexible flex in his own case. There is charm in his answer to Japheth's "You were drunk for nine weeks! Don't *you* ever
get punished?"—"That's special. . . . Sometimes God makes a
little room for human nature." But only if we separate this exchange from his earlier explosion: *"They don't stop acting like
human beings!!"* Nor is it clear in the play that Japheth has "the
true key to man's happiness." He is right about the rudder and
probably about the bride as well, but surely the emphasis on his
similarity to Noah makes the rightness stop there. The word
change runs through the last few scenes like a refrain. God
changes. Noah changes. Presumably Japheth changes as well. If
there is an extractable message it is that yesterday's ideals become this year's rigidities, that a life-giving attitude can harden
into a deadening force. Surely, the implication is that this year's
ideals . . . stay loose, stay loose. The old idealist retires, goes to
live in comfort with the wealthy son, but his blessing ("I pray a
beautiful soul shall enter your baby") goes to the young idealist
and on to his unborn child.

"Yes, something's in the air nowadays . . ." says Goldie when
she arrives in IV, a stranger to the Noah family and its sense of
purpose, "people are troubled, not happy." This suggests the
dislocation and drift of *Night Music* and *Clash by Night,* but a
few reviewers—Thomas R. Dash and Eric Bentley—assumed that
something specific was in the air and pointed to the atom bomb.
Obviously, *Noah's Flood* is a workable image for potential

177

atomic destruction. Such a reading of the play is sanctioned by Rachel's "There is idealism now in just survival," a line that finds its dramatic context in the fact that Japheth and Noah, idealists both, work for survival, finally at the cost of principle. At the end of the play, Noah says, "Yes, I hear you, God—Now it's in man's hands to make or destroy the world." Just before that line he explains to God that the trip has taught him "humility," that he has learned to "listen, even to *myself*." Surely, that line is aimed not only at the Noahs but at their heirs and dispossessors, the Japheths. Odets had moved a long way from the cocksureness of his old political commitment.

Even if the last, atomic step is not taken in the play, it retains a major theme. There remains the problem of whether or not it emerges clearly in *The Flowering Peach*. The reviews suggested that it did not and, even now, I am tempted to agree. The two main problems are the gags and the miracles. In IV, although money will be meaningless in a flooded world, Shem does not want to give up his keys to the tax collector; after Japheth knocks him down and takes them, he struggles to speak. "What, he's saying something?" asks Noah, and Rachel: "He says, 'Get a receipt.'" This joke may be designed to bring the scene back from a moment of high intensity to the family-comedy level on which it has been operating, but it is just as likely to milk away the significance of the Noah-Japheth alliance in the getting of the keys. The presence of God is even more difficult to deal with. He sends thunder in I, a singing gitka (a mouse-like creature, invented by Odets) in II, Noah's youth in IV, a rainbow in IX. Reviewing the play in *Commentary*, I said that it "reduces God to a series of lighting effects by Abe Feder, almost a variation on an offensive old joke: turn on the blue lights, the man wants a blue miracle." Such a reduction is lamentable only if the retelling of the Noah legend attempts to convey the Old Testament God as a reality. This is never the intention of *The Flowering Peach*, although the fact of the Flood may mislead one into assuming that it is. Although I did not recognize it at the time—the *Commentary* lines were meant to be damning—I had stumbled onto an important fact about the play. The miracles are simply recognizable stage effects. This can best be seen at the end of VI, when Noah hides his eyes, not wanting to witness the destruction of his disrespectful family, only to have the sun burst out for the first time since the rain began months before. The very broad gags and the artificial miracles might work theatrically in the "clown" show I suggested earlier in this chapter, but the vaudeville keeps turning into domestic comedy (the too extended wife plot) and that into ideational debate. Such a combination is hardly new to Odets, but it seems peculiarly unmeshed in *The Flowering Peach*. Perhaps a new production would be revealing—one which played down domesticity and debate and let the "clown" show embody the theme.

XVIII. *Don't Blow Bugles*

Is ALL THIS the begining of wisdom or an apology for surrender?" wrote Harold Clurman of the end of *The Flowering Peach*. "Does it bespeak resignation? compromise? defection?" He did not presume to answer his own questions. Perhaps because he had no personal involvement in the playwright, Malcolm Goldstein was less hesitant; he simply assumed that Noah's decision to go with Shem ("It's more comfortable") was Odets's attempt "to explain to himself and to his public the reason for his appearance before the Un-American Activities Committee." Odets did tell Herbert Mitgang that the "meaning of the play is personal to me," and went on to say, "When you start out, you have to champion something. . . . But if you still feel that way after ten or fifteen years, you're nuts."

A simple scenario, then—a 1952 sell-out and a 1954 apologia. Yet, something misgives me in the neatness of it all. Take Goldstein's very direct statement, for instance: "In 1952, following the paths of old friends, Odets took the next step indicated by the fall in his fortunes and made the obligatory trip to Washington for a confession of his political past." In fact, following John Garfield (1951) and Elia Kazan (1952), Odets did appear before the HUAC in executive session on April 24, 1952 and gave public testimony on May 19-20. Yet, "fall in fortune"—after *The Country Girl*, the play that received the success for which it was written? Murray Kempton in *Part of Our Time* said, as though it were an obvious fact, that Odets testified because "the release of his *Clash by Night*" was "at stake." It is true that the movie version of *Clash* was released in June 1952, but Kempton failed to explain why it was "his," what Odets had to gain from the release. He did not write the film; if he had a percentage of it, it is not public knowledge; he was not to work for RKO again and not for Jerry Wald until 1959. Kempton pointed out that "he had begun selling his Paul Klees," but given his divorce from Bette Grayson (November 29, 1951) and California property laws, the selling of his art collection was not necessarily a sign of hard times. If his appearance before the HUAC was simply a matter of looking to his material well-being, why did it take him until 1955 to get back to Hollywood and his presumed rewards? The chronology we do know: after the success of *The Country Girl,* after his divorce, after he directed his former wife in the revival of *Golden Boy,* Odets went through the ritual cleansing before the HUAC. His motivation is less clear, the pay-off not apparent at all. I suspect that it was a complicated set of pressures—personal, political, economic—that sent him to Washington just at the moment when his reputation on Broadway was stronger than it had been since the production of *Golden Boy* in 1937. "Sonafagun!" says Ben Stark at the end of *Rocket to the Moon.* "What I don't know would fill a book!" Although I question the scenario with which I opened this paragraph, I am willing to accept that the last years of Odets—those years of false starts and minimal achievements—date not from the closing of *The Flowering Peach* in 1955, but from the HUAC hearings in 1952.

Yet it was not until *Peach* closed that he went to Hollywood. It was then, he told Lewis Funke, that "I knew I would have to return to California to make a living." Bette Grayson had died in 1954 and with two children to raise, Odets decided it would be easier to live and work on the Coast. One of his first projects was the ill-fated *Joseph and His Brethren.* "Clifford Odets had written what many considered a monumental screenplay," Bob Thomas reported in his biography of Harry Cohn; monumental in size at least, if we are to believe that doubtful reporter, Oscar Levant, who said that the script ran to a thousand pages. Cohn and Columbia finally wrote the project off as a loss.

The first film of this period on which Odets's name appears is *Sweet Smell of Success* (1957), the Hecht-Hill-Lancaster production on which he and Ernest Lehman are listed as co-authors.

According to Lehman, he became so upset during the making of the film that he had to be invalided to Tahiti, and Odets was called in to revise the script. The basic plot and characters are Lehman's—an ambitious publicity man willing to do anything to succeed, the powerful columnist to whom he toadies, and their attempt to break up the romance of the columnist's sister with a young singer. All these are in the Lehman novelette on which the film is based. The young lovers come off more happily in the movie than in the original story, and the come-uppance of the success-and-power villains is manipulated more cleverly—particularly in the case of Sidney, the PR man, who is punished by one of the instruments he uses (the sadistic police lieutenant). There is an attempt to add another dimension to the film by turning Hunsecker—specifically apolitical in the original—into a platitude-spouting, keep-America-pure columnist and commentator, thus suggesting that the corruption is societal as well as personal. Without access to the various versions of the screenplay, it is impossible to assign credit for the changes to either of the co-authors, although the political overtones seem more likely for Odets than Lehman. Certainly, much of the dialogue is Odets's. Lehman, as the novelette indicates, writes the flattest kind of dialogue, only occasionally rising to "Baby" as a noun of address. The tough, funny, metaphorical language of the film ("Watch me run a fifty-yard dash with my legs cut off") has the Odets vitality even when it turns into ludicrous overstatement. One line, at least, is verifiable Odets. At one point the phone rings and Sidney says, "If that's for me, tear it up," a line that Odets used first in *The Silent Partner* and then in *Golden Boy*. The best things about the film are the dialogue and the slick, sleazy look of New York at night that James Wong Howe gets in his photography. The serious implications of the script are lost in the plot and the characterization of Hunsecker, whom Robert Hatch identified, aptly, as "the mad scientist of the side-street horror movies." Odets has used grotesques before, but Hunsecker's mannerisms seem not to grow out of his social function (as Hoff's did in *The Big Knife*) but out of his incestuous love for his sister. *Sweet Smell of Success*, as a cautionary tale, was crippled by staying too close to its source.

Odets's next film was *The Story on Page One* (1960), which he

wrote and directed for producer Jerry Wald at 20th Century
Fox. "You can do almost anything you want in Hollywood, providing you're a good writer," Odets told Murray Schumach, in
one of his occasional bursts of enthusiasm for the film industry.
"You can say almost anything within reason." In the face of
such promise, *Page One* is a disappointment. It is a story of
infidelity, murder and true love which fails to be several
different movies at once. It is a reasonably exciting courtroom
drama in which the villainous assistant district attorney (Sanford
Meisner, Odets's old Group Theatre associate, being comically
hissable) is bested by the personable young lawyer, who saves
the falsely accused lovers by forcing the man's possessive mother
to break down on the stand. There is the love story which attempts to deal simply with an affair between two unhappy people and which defeats itself by a too-deliberate understatement
that gives it the look of a television serial. There is the tale of
two mothers which Stanley Kauffmann admired, but both
women are caricatures with no clear thematic function, operating only within the plot. There is the social play which dies
a-borning. At the beginning of the film, the young lawyer explains the economic facts of life—that only the well-off stand a
chance against a state more interested in conviction than in
justice—but the facts of movie life contradict him by letting him
save the poor heroine before the film ends. Any social implication in the title (and the press run that follows hard on the cred-
its) is highly peripheral since the movie does not treat the very
real problem of trial by newspaper. There is the tactile film
(James Wong Howe again) which, outside the courtroom, fo-
cuses on the tacky texture of houses and furniture, inelegant
offices, neighborhood bars. As the reviewer in *The Reporter*
pointed out, this is an approximation of the quasi-documentary
style popular right after World War II of which *Boomerang*
(1947), directed by another Group alumnus, Elia Kazan, is the
best example. There is something attractive about an attempt to
make that kind of movie in 1960, but Odets's good intentions
were finally crushed by courtroom conventionality and the soap-
iness of the love affair. *The Story on Page One* is, sadly, a dull
movie.

Odets's last film—also for Wald—was *Wild in the Country*

(1961), a vehicle for Elvis Presley. Philip Dunne directed. This was before the string of song anthologies in which Presley starred, when there was still hope in Hollywood for him as an actor; so a character of a sort was required. Based very distantly on *The Lost Country*, J. R. Salamanca's relentlessly overwritten but interesting novel about growing up, *Wild* is a conventional story of a tough, sensitive victim of circumstances who drags his guitar, his guilt and his priapus through a field of three ladies before settling with the older woman who almost succeeds in committing suicide because of the sadness of it all. She is the one who recognizes his writing talent: "Glenn, have you any idea how good this is?" There are recognizable Odets lines (one, "Everything with a kiss," borrowed inappropriately from *None But the Lonely Heart*) among the bromides, but most of the script could have been written by any of the Hollywood regulars. Most of the reviewers simply ignored Odets's connection with the film, but Bosley Crowther mourned: "alas, Mr. Odets."

At the end of his life, Odets was at work on two projects. One was the musical version of *Golden Boy* which, rewritten by William Gibson, was produced in 1964. The other was *The Richard Boone Show*, a television drama series. According to Odets, it was Jean Renoir who tempted him by touting the virtues of TV as a popular medium and Boone who sold him with "Don't you realize that together, with a hand-picked company of players, that we probably can make the first real theatre on TV?" Between the bottle of wine with Renoir and the business meeting with Boone came, presumably, Goodson-Todman Productions which brought author and actor together and which, with Odets, formed Classic Films, co-owner with NBC of the series. The company consisted of ten performers besides the star, who were to appear in large or small parts as the particular script demanded. A distant mass-media echo of the Group Theatre—no wonder Odets was interested. He was to write four of the thirteen scripts and, as editor-in-chief, supervise all of them. "To hell with the astronauts. To hell with the moon," he told a *Time* interviewer. "There's a whole sky in your chest that's waiting to be explored." The sentence implies that Odets, the social dramatist, is set to plumb the depths of personal experience, but it can serve as well as an image of the withdrawal into the small, easily encompassable subject matter suitable to the medium, the time limitations, the mass audience.

Two Odets scripts were performed—*Big Mitch* (December 10, 1963) and *The Mafia Man* (January 7, 1964). The first of these, originally called *North Star* (the trade name of the freezer in the script), is about a man who lives on unemployment insurance and expectations, talking of big deals in the offing, who makes a grand gesture—the gift freezer—when his daughter marries and who is forced finally to take a job to keep up the payments. The play ends with a tentative bridging of the gulf that pride has cut between him and the married couple and a close-up of Mitch which is supposed to tell the audience where its sentiments should lie. "Quite a face on the man," reads the stage direction. The second script, originally called *Don't Blow Bugles,* is about a ganster who agrees to return to the United States to testify against his colleagues if he is given a chance to reassure his son who, shocked by the scandal, has lost his "attitude to live;" at the end of the play, the hero is cheerfully bleeding to death in a cocktail lounge as he watches his son smilingly welcome the spunky girl whom the father met on the plane. Both scripts are simple character turns, designed for a final lump in the throat. A third script, variously called *The Affair* and *The Nursery,* was never done. In some ways, it is the most interesting of the three. Less slick than the other two, perhaps because it was not revised, it misleadingly presents its protagonist as a sullen, suspicious husband; his motivation is belatedly revealed in a final scene in the nursery of his dead son. The points that the play wants to make—that grief and the pain of infidelity must be shared and that psychoanalysis, by relieving one half the couple, is a dangerously excluding process—are more ambitious than the simple, anecdotal statements about pride and family in *Big Mitch* and *The Mafia Man*.

By the time *The Richard Boone Show* made its debut, Clifford Odets was dead. He was admitted to the Cedars of Lebanon hospital on July 23, 1963, to undergo an operation for ulcers. He died of cancer on August 14.

From time to time during the last eight years of his life Odets sent out signals implying that there was a dramatist still alive out there on the West Coast. "I've been read off as a dead writer ten times in ten years," he told Joe Hyams, "and the critics are always surprised when I come back." In the 1962 Lewis Funke interview quoted earlier in this chapter, Odets mentioned by title four plays he was working on. It was little more than a gesture. Odets had always sprinkled his interviews with projected plays, ideas taking shape, works in progress. Too often, presumably, he failed to find that necessary "psychological boost" he mentioned in the Elliot Norton interview about *The Country Girl*. "In the course of our relationship," wrote Hillard Elkins, who produced the musical *Golden Boy*, "Clifford had periods of tremendous creativity, but always he slipped back into the bog of self-doubt." "Although he was always full of ideas for plays and blandly convinced of his own genius," wrote Brooks Atkinson in his obituary article on Odets, "he was unable to accept the harsh disciplines of writing and staging plays on Broadway." The point of the Atkinson piece was that Odets was a man of many interests, too easily side-tracked to be a devoted worker, that he was not so much the failed playwright that most of the obituaries clucked over as a successful person. That is a nice, gentle way of marking a death, rounding off a life with a final fade-out as consoling as the end of *Big Mitch* or *The Mafia Man*.

Those last eight years, whatever comfort Odets may have found in them, were empty ones for the playwright. Yet, with Atkinson if not for his reasons, I am ready to discard the failed-dramatist cliché. Odets left a body of work—flawed and imperfect as it is—that from *Waiting for Lefty* to *The Flowering Peach* shows him as one of our most talented playwrights. Although Elmer Rice harked back to the excitement of 1935 in his presentation speech, it was for Odets's work as a whole that the playwright received the Award of Merit Medal for Drama from the American Academy of Arts and Letters on May 24, 1961. Characteristically, in his acceptance statement, Odets was looking toward the future.

Afterword

Mr. Bonaparte was wrong and so was Marion Castle. No man is so simply made that he has a single nature which a wrong turn can violate. The violation, too, is in his nature. Both fist and fiddle were natural to Joe; both Hollywood and the escape from it were necessary to Charlie. The observer in Odets knew this; the idealist, the idealogue did not want to know. Alter the circumstances, rearrange the environment, brick off the false choices, said the latter, and the natural man will flower; home, love, happiness will become possible. This assumption had personal and artistic consequences for Odets.

He was a restless man. In his work and in his life, we can see the vacillation between a home which turns out to be a trap and a promised land that fails to keep its promises. That comic figure, the radical playwright in the fashionable Hollywood restaurant, is an oblique image for the artist who never found consolation in his art. The idealist in Odets could point Ralph toward the future, but the observer in him, who could see the self-pity and the weakness in the character, also knew that the making of *Awake and Sing!* did not bring peace. Odets did what was "ina [his] nature to do" and it was not enough. He ran, in disappointment, to Hollywood and ran back, in guilt, to the stage. "A job is a home to a homeless man," says Bernie in *The Country Girl*, but he is looking around for a real home or its equivalent in

187

Georgie. Odets was still coping with the homelessness of art at the end of his life. He told Michael J. Mendelsohn that he wanted to write a play about the Biblical David: "And I want to show the life of Man from the time he is a poet until he died an old man, unhappy, but somehow still a poet gnawing at his soul." In an odd piece he wrote for *Show,* half fiction, half sociology, the profile of a mythical movie star, Odets quoted his friend Jean Renoir. The lines are aimed at the actor, but since he is Odets's invention, it is safe to assume that they were at some time spoken to the inventor himself: "Maybe, my friend, when you were given so many other gifts, you must grow used to the fact that happiness is not among them."

The artistic consequences of Odets's ideational approach to man are less conjectural than the personal ones. The plays are their own testimony. "I believe in the vast potentialities of mankind . . ." Odets wrote to John Mason Brown back in 1935. "I want to find out how mankind can be helped out of the animal kingdom into the clear sweet air." The rhetoric may be a little heady (Odets was only twenty-nine), but the line contains a statement of artistic intentions that can be tested in all of Odets's plays. The "how" is finally less important than that there be a way into the "clear sweet air." From the certainty of *Waiting for Lefty* to the uncertainty of *The Flowering Peach,* Odets has organized his plays to make a specific point about human possibility; he has manipulated his characters to let one or more of them reach the moment of change, of recognition that will allow the play to look into a better future. A propagandist, first and last, he has always held out hope of the happy land. It is this quality that makes Odets such a likable playwright, since a happy ending (even if it is a tragic one) is hard to resist. The same quality limits him as a playwright, threatens to reduce him to the simplicity of his ideas, his themes. Yet the observer in Odets never let the preacher run free, the pessimist hobbled the optimist, the realist partnered the idealist. Although the discussions of the plays in this book tend—as such discussions always do—to bring the order of argument to the multiplicity of art, they are sprinkled with a "yes-but" hesitation which indicates that the characters, the dramatic situations, the lines slip their traces and escape their functions within the ideational drama. From Bessie Berger to Noah, the characters refuse to stay nailed down. Villains start charming us, heroes turn into milksops, minor characters stroll across stage and walk off with the play. I sort out the symbols in *Golden Boy* only to discover that my mind's eye is on Roxy in I, 3, where, having made a mess of things as usual by shooting off his mouth, he says, "What's the matter? What happened?" and shrugging, "I think I'll run across the street and pick up an eight-cylinder lunch." I satisfy myself about the use of the Washington-Lincoln motif in *Night Music*, but the concept is upstaged by the hot-fur salesman in I, 2: "Take it for ten plus ten—that's what I'll do—two ten spots an' you can't go wrong." The contrast between the simplicity of concept and the complexity of creation which in the man himself must have caused pain and unrest, in the plays brought richness. Odets's plays have a way of being less than what the perfectionist in us wants them to be, but they are a great deal more than they seem to the jaundiced eye.

A last word? A summing up? A final epigrammatic sentence that reduces the troubled artist to a neat label?

Well, why not? Here are two. Choose the one you like.

Peter Bogdanovich met Odets two years after he had directed the off-Broadway revival of *The Big Knife* and asked him why he had given a nineteen-year-old enthusiast permission to put on his play. Odets answered, "I took a drop in the ocean."

At the end of *The Flowering Peach*, having accepted God's convenant and delivered the playwright's message to the audience, Noah looks up and says, "I'll tell you a mystery."

Notes on Sources

T HE ITEMS in the biblioclots that follow are not formal foot-note references. They simply list the sources of quotations and unusual bits of information not identified in the text. They will be of interest only to those readers who want to check my assumptions or pursue a particular subject further. The entries are as short as possible. The New York City newspapers are identified by title only (*Sun* rather than New York *Sun*); other newspapers carry the city name unless it is already in the text. Except for a rare item, publication information on the books cited seemed unnecessary in this context.

Chapter I.
Liebling, *World-Telegram,* April 6, 1935; Odets interview, *Harper's,* September 1966; Ross, *World-Telegram,* September 20, 1935; *Town and Country,* March 15, 1935; MacLeish, *New Theatre,* August 1935; *Times* interview, May 3, 1936; Nathan, *Vogue,* March, 1936; *New Yorker,* January 22, 1938; *Time,* December 5, 1938; Vernon, *Commonweal,* June 10, 1938; Gassner, *Theatre at the Crossroads;* Baltimore *Sun,* October 27, 1941.

Chapter II.
Sugrue, *American Magazine,* October 1936; HUAC, May 19-20, 1952; Odets, as worker's son, *Time,* December 5, 1938; McCarten, *New Yorker,* January 22, 1938; Odets admission, *Current Biography,* 1941; Philadelphia *Record,* March 31, 1935; Peck, *Times,* February 20, 1949; Clurman, *Times,* August 25, 1963; Powell, Philadelphia *Ledger,* March 18,

1938; *Record*, October 3, 1935; Odets disc jockey claim, *World-Telegram*, January 10, 1949; Odets actor's application, *World-Telegram*, May 26, 1938; Mantle, *Contemporary American Playwrighters;* Hammond, *Herald Tribune*, December 30, 1930; Mantle, *Daily News*, May 12, 1933; Lockridge, *Sun*, May 12, 1933; Pollock, Brooklyn *Eagle*, May 12, 1933; L.N., *Times*, May 12, 1933; Atkinson, *Times*, February 11, 1935; *Eagle*, August 4, 1935; Cohan, *Post*, March 24, 1936; Stanislavsky, Clurman, *Theatre Arts*, November 1935; Odets on suicide and particular chums, *Harper's*, September, 1966; Clurman, *Saturday Review*, September 14, 1963; Adler, in Leonard Lyons, *Post*, August 16, 1963; Mendelsohn, *Theatre Arts*, May, 1963; Thacher, *New Theatre*, July-August 1934; Odets, on Group influence, *Harper's;* Mantle, *Contemporary American Playwrights;* Odets descriptions of prose work in Mantle, *Contemporary*, and *Harper's;* organ quote, *Daily News*, January 10, 1937; letter to Dreiser, December 31, 1935, Dreiser Collection, University of Pennsylvania; Odets boast, *Time;* Mendelsohn, *Clifford Odets: Humane Dramatist; General* quote, *Stage*, October 1936.

Chapter III.
Contest, *New Theatre*, September 1934, *New Masses*, September 18, 1934; Odets, HUAC, May 19-20, 1952; Kazan, HUAC, April 10, 1952; Odets persuading Smith, *Harper's*, September 1966; Odets suggestion, Thomas Sugrue, *American Magazine*, October 1936; Odets admission, *Harper's;* Norton, Boston *Post*, February 11, 1940; Adler, Clurman, *The Fervent Years;* Buchwald, *Worker*, January 12, 1935; Odets on Strasberg, *Harper's;* Burnshaw, *New Masses*, January 29, 1935; Mendelsohn, *Theatre Arts*, May 1963; Eliot, *Poetry and Drama;* Garland, *World-Telegram*, February 20, 1935; *Stage*, March 1935; Maltz, *New Republic*, July 24, 1935; Odets, *New Theatre*, January 1936; Davis, *Time*, June 15, 1935; Pack, in *Censored!*, pamphlet published by the National Committee Against Censorship of the Theatre Arts, New York, 1935; Mantle, *Daily News*, July 7, 1935; *Lefty* story, *Times*, February 20, 1938; taxi strike, *Times*, March 21, 1934; LaGuardia warns, *Times*, March 23; LaGuardia implies, *Times*, March 24; Orner denial, *Times*, March 19; Orner's brave mouth, *Times*, April 1; expulsion, *Times*, April 13; Odets, *Worker*, March 27, 1935; *New Masses* on textile strike, October 2, 1934; *Nation*, August 1, 1934; Adamic, *New Republic*, July 4, 1934; second textile strike article, *New Masses*, also October 2; Shulman, *Call*, April 6, 1935; Shipley, *New Leader*, March 30, 1935; Klein, *New Leader*, March 16, 1935; *Worker*, March 27, 1935; Odets admits agitprop form, *Harper's;* conference report, *Workers Theatre*, May 1932; Krutch, *Nation*, April 10, 1935; Pottle, *Yale Review*, Winter 1936; Deutsch, *Herald Tribune*, April 28, 1935; Brown, *Post*, March 27, 1935; photograph, *Literary Digest*, April 6, 1935, original in Theatre Collection, New York Public Library; Lawson, *Theory and Technique of Playwriting;* Mendelsohn, *Theatre Arts*, June 1963.

Chapter IV.
Unless otherwise identified, all Odets recollections in this chapter are from *Harper's*, September 1966.
Odets, *World-Telegram*, March 19, 1935; Clurman, *Herald Tribune*, March 10, 1935; *Awake* listing, *Times*, November 27, 1933; Isaacs, *Theatre Arts*, April 1939; Buchwald, *Worker*, February 20, 1935; Winchell, *Mirror*, February 20, 1935; Lawson, *Theory and Technique of Playwriting;* Dean, *Georges Bizet, His Life and Work;* Gilder, *Theatre Arts*, May 1939; Warshow, *The Immediate Experience;* Odets interviews, *Herald Tribune*, February 17, 1935, *Mirror*, February 25; Mantle, *Daily News*, February 20, 1935; Bolton, as John Whitney, Newark *News*, February 20, 1935; Morris, *Postscript to Yesterday;* Cuban Tourist Commission, *Times*, February 10, 1934; police announcement, *Times*, November 27, 1934; Odets interview, *Times*, May 3, 1936; Odets defending end of *Awake*, *Theatre Arts*, May 1963; Farmer, *New Theatre*, March 1935; Garland, *World-Telegram*, February 20, 1935; Stein, *Post*, April 12, 1935; Carnovsky, Brooklyn *Eagle*, February 17, 1935; Young, *New Republic*, May 29, 1935; Burnshaw, *New Masses*, January 29, 1935; Clurman adjectives, *Times*, August 25, 1963; Clurman nouns, Introduction, *Famous American Plays of the 1930s;* Ferguson, *New Republic*, September 27, 1939.

Chapter V.
Watts, *Herald Tribune*, March 31, 1935; Isaacs, *Theatre Arts*, May 1935; *Variety*, May 29, 1935; Lockridge, *Sun*, March 27, 1935; Odets on letter, *Harper's*, September 1966; Weiskopf story, *New Masses*, November 6, 1934; Farrell, *Partisan Review and Anvil*, February 1936; Atkinson, *Times*, March 27, 1935; Shulman, *Call*, April 6, 1935; Lewis's make-up, Helen Deutsch, *Herald Tribune*, April 28, 1935; Alexander, *Worker*, April 1, 1935; Hammond, *Herald Tribune*, April 7, 1935; Wittenberg, *New Theatre*, April 1935.

Chapter VI.
Odets on *Paradise*, *Harper's*, September 1966; Mantle, *Contemporary American Playwrights;* Odets, *Times*, December 15, 1935; Krutch, *Nation*, December 25, 1935; Krutch's answer to Clurman, *Nation*, January 1, 1936; Odets interview, *Journal*, May 29, 1936; Burnshaw, *New Masses*, February 11, 1936; Atkinson, *Times*, December 29, 1935; Brown, *Post*, January 4, 1936; Broun, *World-Telegram*, December 18, 1935; Fadiman, *Stage*, February 1936; Garland, *World-Telegram*, December 14, 1935; Watts, *Herald Tribune*, December 22, 1935; Odets originals, dated December 31, 14, 26, 1935, and Dreiser carbons, dated December 23, 27, in Dreiser Collection, University of Pennsylvania; YMHA forum, January 30, 1936; Clurman, *New Theatre*, January 1936; Lockridge, *Sun*, December 10, 1935; Gold, *New Masses*, February 18, 1936; Gassner, *New Theatre*, January 1936; Odets recollection, *Harper's;*

Odets interview, *World-Telegram*, December 8, 1935; Lockridge, *Sun*, December 14, 1935; Brecht letter, *Progressive Labor*, December, 1965; editorial, *New Masses*, July 2, 1935; Garland, *op. cit.*; Bagley, *Worker*, February 16, 1936; Farrell, *Partisan Review and Anvil*, February, 1936; Burke, *New Republic*, April 15, 1936.

Chapter VII.
Sugrue, *American Magazine*, October 1936; Odets, HUAC, May 19-20, 1952; Kazan, HUAC, April 10, 1952; Burnshaw, *New Masses*, January 29, 1935; Buchwald, *Worker*, February 20, 1935; Blankfort, *New Masses*, March 5, 1935; Farmer, *New Theatre*, March 1935; Biberman & Blankfort's answer, *New Masses*, March 26, 1935; Farrell letter, *New Theatre*, June 1935; Aaron, *Writers on the Left*; Blankfort, HUAC, January 28, 1952; Brecht letter, dated February 1936, *Progressive Labor*, December, 1965; Odets on Caffrey, *News*, July 7, 1935; *Journal*, July 6, 1935; *Post*, July 5, 1935, reprinted, Philadelphia *Record*, July 6; Odets, *New Masses*, July 16, 1935; *Times*, July 24, 1935; *World-Telegram*, July 26, 1935; Rabkin, *Drama and Commitment*; Rappaport, *New Theatre*, December 1935; McCarten, *New Yorker*, January 22, 1938.

Chapter VIII.
Flying Grouse, February 1936; Odets interview, *Herald Tribune*, July 18, 1936; Mendelsohn, *Theatre Arts*, June 1963; Watts, *Herald Tribune*, November 13, 1935; Odets quote, *Record*, March 22, 1936; Clurman recollection, *Times*, August 25, 1963; Odets on Hollywood fraud, *Times*, May 3, 1936; Gabriel, *American*, February 20, 1935; Ross, *World-Telegram*, February 28, 1935; Milestone, *Stage*, October 1936; Nugent, *Times*, September 6, 1936; Kaufman, *New Masses*, July 28, 1936; Stebbins, *New Theatre*, October 1936; Odets on *General*, *Harper's*, September 1966; Winchell column for March 28, 1936; Odets, HUAC, May 19-20, 1952; Lawson, *Film: The Creative Process*; *Times*, December 18, 1936; Hall, *Photoplay*, March 1937; Hall, *Journal*, January 23, 1937; Parsons, *Journal-American*, July 3, 1938; *Daily News*, January 10, 1937.

Chapter IX.
Daily News, September 10, 1936; *Sun*, October 6, 1936; Stein, *Post*, April 24, 1936; *Partner* report, *World-Telegram*, November 26, 1935; Odets, *Harper's*, September 1966; McCarten, *New Yorker*, January 22, 1938; Odets defense, *World-Telegram*, December 3, 1938; Odets "five of . . .," *Harper's*; *Flight* information, *Herald Tribune*, July 18, 1936.

Chapter X.
Odets, *Harper's*, September 1966; Coleman, *Mirror*, April 5, 1938; Paxton, *Stage*, December 1938; Mendelsohn, *Theatre Arts*, May 1963; Mantle, *Daily News*, November 5, 1937; Dexter, *Worker*, November 12,

1937; Odets, *Times,* November 21, 1937; Pascar, *Figaro,* December 20, 1938; Lockridge, *Sun,* November 5, 1937; Seldes, *Atlantic Monthly,* January 1938.

Chapter XI.
Odets, *World-Telegram,* December 3, 1938; Wolfert, Providence *Journal,* December 4, 1938; Pollock, Brooklyn *Eagle,* December 4, 1938; Lockridge, *Sun,* January 28, 1939; *Home News,* November 25, 1938.

Chapter XII.
Mantle, *Daily News,* February 23, 1940; Bessie, *New Masses,* February 20, 1940; Shipley, *New Leader,* March 16, 1940; Clurman on revival, *New Republic,* April 30, 1951; Clurman, *Times,* March 3, 1940; Atkinson, *Times,* February 23, 1940; Dusenbury, *The Theme of Loneliness in Modern American Drama;* Gilder, *Theatre Arts,* April 1940; Krutch, *Nation,* March 2, 1940; Bessie on Steve, *New Masses,* March 5, 1940; Anderson, *Journal-American,* February 23, 1940; Eager, *Traveller,* February 9, 1940; Gorelik, *Theatre Arts,* March 1939; Gorelik on slides, letter, August 11, 1969; Bowles, *TAC Magazine,* March 15, 1940; Odets interview, *New York Times Magazine,* March 31, 1940.

Chapter XIII.
Odets journal, *Times,* February 1, 1942; Mantle, *Daily News,* March 11, 1941; *Record,* November 18, 1941; Morehouse, *Sun,* February 18; 1949; *Variety,* February 11, 1942; Beebe, *Herald Tribune,* January 4, 1942; McLaughlin, Detroit *News,* October 28, 1941; Rabkin, *Drama and Commitment;* Anderson, *Journal-American,* December 29, 1941, January 4, 1942; Bohnen, *Times,* January 15, 1942.

Chapter XIV.
Peck, *Times,* February 20, 1949; USSR Embassy *Information Bulletin,* December 12, 1942; Mendelsohn, *Theatre Arts,* May 1963; Rascoe, *World-Telegram,* December 30, 1942; Pollock, Brooklyn *Eagle,* December 30, 1942; Morehouse, *Sun,* February 18, 1949; *Variety,* March 2, 1949; Stieglitz letters, Beinecke Library, Yale University; Grant, *Ladies' Home Journal,* March 1963; Farber, *New Republic,* December 11, 1944; *Time,* November 20, 1944; Rogers, HUAC, October 24, 1947; Odets letter, *Time,* December 1, 1947; Agee, *Nation,* December 2, 1944; *Newsweek,* December 23, 1946; Levant, *The Memoirs of an Amnesiac;* Wilson, Philadelphia *Bulletin,* February 13, 1947; *PM,* February 9, 1947.

Chapter XV.
Odets on 2 kinds of play-writing, *Times,* April 22, 1951; *Variety,* February 2, 1949; Hughes, Boston *Herald,* Norton, Boston *Post,* February 13, 1949; second *Variety* review, March 2, 1949; Ross, *New Yorker,* May 24, 1952; Odets on movie *Knife, Times,* November 6, 1955; Odets

on title change, *Herald Tribune*, May 1, 1949; Morehouse, *Sun*, February 18, 1949; Pollock, Brooklyn *Eagle*, May 17, 1936; Odets quote, *Variety*, March 2, 1949; Mendelsohn, *Theatre Arts*, June 1963.

Chapter XVI.
The play was published in *Theatre Arts*, May 1952, with comments by Odets and others involved in the production. Unless otherwise identified, the Odets quotations in the chapter are from that source.
Odets interview, *Bulletin*, March 19, 1953; Odets dismisses *Girl*, *Theatre Arts*, May 1963; Atkinson, *Times*, November 19, 1950; Odets interview, *Herald Tribune*, November 5, 1950; Norton, *Times*, November 5, 1950; Haring, *Theatre Arts*, May 1952; Atkinson, *Times*, November 11, 1950; Odets on title, *Herald Tribune*, May 1, 1949; Coleman, *Mirror*, November 11, 1950; Watts, *Post*, November 12, 1950; Brown, *Saturday Review of Literature*, December 9, 1950; Hagen interview, *Herald Tribune*, February 25, 1951; Clurman, *Lies Like Truth;* Gassner, *Theatre at the Crossroads;* Kerr, *Commonweal*, December 1, 1950.

Chapter XVII.
Opera information, Odets interview, Herbert Mitgang, *Times*, December 26, 1954; Hughes, Boston *Herald*, December 7, 1954; Campbell, *Times*, August 18, 1963; see Mitgang for originals of Noah and Esther; Kerr, *Herald Tribune*, January 16, 1955; Dash, *Women's Wear Daily*, December 29, 1954; Bentley, *New Republic*, January 10, 1955; Weales, *Commentary*, July 1955.

Chapter XVIII.
Clurman, *Lies Like Truth;* Goldstein, in Alan S. Downer, *American Drama and Its Critics;* Mitgang, *Times*, December 26, 1954; Funke, *Times*, July 8, 1962; Thomas, *King Cohn;* Levant, *The Memoirs of an Amnesiac;* Lehman, *Times*, November 24, 1968; Hatch, *Nation*, July 20, 1957; Schumach, *Times*, October 1, 1959; Kauffmann, *New Republic*, February 8, 1960; *Reporter*, February 18, 1960; Crowther, *Times*, June 10, 1961; Odets tempted by Jean Renoir, Los Angeles *Times*, August 1, 1963; *Time*, December 14, 1962; Hyams, *Herald Tribune*, September 10, 1959; Norton, *Times*, November 5, 1950; Elkins, *Philadelphia Inquirer Magazine*, June 14, 1964; Atkinson, *Times*, September 3, 1963.

Afterword
Mendelsohn, *Theatre Arts*, May 1963; Odets, *Show*, April 1963; Brown, *Post*, April 5, 1935; Bogdanovich, *Times*, September 15, 1968.

Select Bibliography

Titles marked (OP) are out of print and not available in other editions.

PRIMARY SOURCES

(a) Plays

Six Plays. New York, Grove, 1979. London, Methuen, 1982. Contains *Waiting for Lefty* (short version), *Awake and Sing!*, *Till the Day I Die, Paradise Lost, Golden Boy* and *Rocket to the Moon*.

Waiting for Lefty (complete version), *Representative Modern Plays: American*, ed. Robert Warnock, Chicago, Scott Foresman, 1952.

Night Music. New York, Random House, 1940. (OP)

Clash by Night. New York, Random House, 1942. (OP)

The Big Knife. New York, Random House, 1949. Acting edition available, Dramatists Play Service, New York.

The Country Girl. New York, Viking, 1951. As *Winter Journey*, London, French, 1955. Acting edition available, Dramatists Play Service, New York.

The Flowering Peach. Acting edition available, Dramatists Play Service, New York.

(b) Film scripts, sketches, adaptations

"I Can't Sleep," *New Theatre*, 3 (February, 1936), 8–9.

Excerpts from *The General Died at Dawn* in Sidney Kaufman, "Odets's First Film," *New Masses*, 20 (July 28, 1936), 12–13.

One scene from *The Silent Partner*, *New Theatre*, 4 (March, 1937), 5–9.

The Russian People in *Seven Soviet Plays*, ed. H. W. L. Dana, New York, Macmillan, 1946. (OP) American acting version of Konstantin Simonov's *The Russians*.

None But the Lonely Heart in *Best Film Plays—1945*, ed.

John Gassner and Dudley Nichols, New York, Garland, 1973.

Clifford Odets and William Gibson, *Golden Boy*, New York, Atheneum, 1965. (OP) The book of the musical version; although Odets's name is on the title page, the work is primarily Gibson's.

SELECTED SECONDARY WORKS

Bentley, Eric (ed.), *Thirty Years of Treason*. New York, Viking, 1971. (OP) Contains testimony of Odets and Elia Kazan before House Un-American Activities Committee.

Brenman-Gibson, Margaret, *Clifford Odets, American Playwright*. New York, Atheneum, 1981. Contains otherwise unavailable material from diaries and letters.

Clurman, Harold, *The Fervent Years*. New York, Da Capo, 1983. Originally published in 1945 by Knopf.

Lewis, Robert, *Slings and Arrows*. New York, Stein and Day, 1984.

Mendelsohn, Michael J., "Odets at Center Stage," *Theatre Arts*, 47 (May, 1963), 16–19, 74–76; (June, 1963), 28–30, 78–80. Interview.

Murray, Edward, *Clifford Odets: The Thirties and After*. New York, Ungar, 1968.

Odets, Clifford, "How a Playwright Triumphs," *Harper's*, 233 (September, 1966), 64–74. Invented article, drawn from interviews Arthur Wagner conducted over two days in 1961.

Shuman, R. Baird, *Clifford Odets*. New York, Twayne, 1962.

Other articles by and about Odets and interviews with him are identified in the Notes on Sources.

Index

INDEX

INDEX

INDEX

202

INDEX

INDEX